GAME CHANGERS

The Greatest Plays in
Buffalo Bills
Football History

Marv Levy with Jeff Miller

TRIUMPH
BOOKS

*To those incomparable Buffalo Bills fans who have supplied so much of the excitement and support
that kept me motivated during my never-to-be-forgotten 12 years in Buffalo. —Marv Levy*

*To my parents, Joe and Dottie Miller, both of whom left this world while this book was being written. I miss you very much.
And to my wife Cathaline and our beautiful son Benjamin, who have supported me throughout this project with their
unwavering encouragement, understanding, and patience. Love you both! —Jeff Miller*

Library of Congress Cataloging-in-Publication Data

Levy, Marv.
  Game changers : the greatest plays in Buffalo Bills history / Marv Levy with Jeff Miller.
      p. cm.
  Includes bibliographical references.
  ISBN 978-1-60078-275-6
  1. Buffalo Bills (Football team)—History. I. Miller, Jeff II. Title.
  GV956.B83L48 2009
  796.332'640974797—dc22

                    2009029651

This book is available in quantity at special discounts for your group or organization. For further
information, contact:
  Triumph Books
  542 South Dearborn Street
  Suite 750
  Chicago, Illinois 60605
  (312) 939-3330
  Fax (312) 663-3557
  www.triumphbooks.com

Printed in U.S.A.
ISBN: 978-1-60078-275-6
Design by Sue Knopf/Patricia Frey
Page production by Patricia Frey
Photos courtesy of Getty Images unless otherwise indicated

Contents

Acknowledgments   iv

Introduction   v

Chapter 1: Offensive Wonders   1

Chapter 2: Game-Winning Touchdowns   39

Chapter 3: Defensive Standouts   73

Chapter 4: Special Teams Heroics   111

Chapter 5: Memorable Moments   141

Bibliography   154

Acknowledgments

Thanks to the Buffalo Bills Media Relations Department, headed by Scott Berchtold. Their work, as always, was fantastic. The members of the department who provided so much help include Dawn Dotzler, Chris Jenkins, Matt Heidt, and Dominick Rinelli. Thanks also to Jeff Miller, whose role in steering the ship was invaluable.

—Marv Levy

Thanks to Bob Carroll, executive director of the Professional Football Researchers Association and author of *When the Grass Was Real*; John Maxymuk, author of several football books, including *The 50 Greatest Plays in New York Giants Football History*; Dan Dilandro and Peggy Hatfield at the Butler Library at Buffalo State College; and Denny Lynch, archivist for the Buffalo Bills (retired). Thanks also to Craig Irish, Robert Kaiser, Jeffrey Mason, and Joseph F. Miller Jr., all of whom offered help and support during this project. Special thanks to the members of the Buffalo Bills family who loaned their voices to this project, including Eddie Abramoski, Al Bemiller, Butch Byrd, Booker Edgerson, Charley Ferguson, George Flint, Harry Jacobs, Jack Kemp, Joe O'Donnell, Ed Rutkowski, Lou Saban, Billy Shaw, Roy S. Sheppard, and Mike Stratton.

I'd also like to express my undying gratitude to Adam Motin, Tom Bast, and all of the professionals at Triumph Books.

And to Marv Levy—it's been both a privilege and a pleasure working with you.

—Jeff Miller

Introduction

Alex Webster, a star player with the New York Giants in the 1950s and 1960s and later an outstanding announcer for Giants games, was once asked what individual played the most important role in determining how successful an NFL team would be. Was it the quarterback? Was it the team captain? Was it the general manager? Was it the coach? C'mon, who was it?

"None of those," Alex responded. "The most important one is the team's owner." I was fortunate enough to have been in a position to offer my personal validation for Alex's astute observation, because during the 12 years that I served as coach of the Buffalo Bills, I, and everyone who worked with me, had the privilege of observing what Bills owner and founder Ralph Wilson brought not only to our team but also what he contributed to the community, to the fans, and to the immense success and popularity that the NFL has enjoyed.

In this book, I recall some glorious days that I shared with some wondrous people during my years as coach of the team. Jeff Miller, with whom I collaborated in the writing of this book, recounts many of the exciting events that helped to shape the earlier years prior to my tenure as the team's coach, and then he details a few more that occurred since that day I left the sideline. Through all of these ups and downs over the half-century since our Buffalo Bills players first sprinted out onto the playing field, there has been one person who remains unique even among the many personalities that comprise the history of this team. That person, of course, is Ralph Wilson.

It was 50 years ago that the Buffalo Bills first came into being as a member of the American Football League. Today the team remains in its original city with the same dedicated owner still at the helm. No other team in the NFL today can make that assertion.

Ralph Wilson's loyalty to the fans of Buffalo and the surrounding areas is unparalleled, and part of the reason for that is because of how deserving those Buffalo Bills fans are. Take it from a man who knows. Take it from a man who is so proud to say, "I worked for (make that 'worked with') Ralph Wilson and with those Buffalo Bills fans."

It was my good fortune to have been part of a shining era in Buffalo Bills history, but I also know, of some never-to-be-forgotten moments in the years that preceded—and then those that followed—my days as coach of the team. Still living in the Buffalo area are many of the players who played for the Bills in the years before I came there. It has been my pleasure to get to know and to visit with them on numerous occasions. Hearing them—and some of the older fans whose hair color approximates mine—recount their experiences in the old War Memorial Stadium (to which they refer affectionately as "the Rockpile") may get repetitious at times, but never boring.

In this book, Jeff and I recall exciting plays, ones which were integral in shaping the team's history. I'll remember them, but even more, I'll remember the people that made it all happen. Players, coaches, fans, and people who worked in sometimes obscure roles in the Buffalo Bills organization all helped to shape what you will read about in the pages that follow.

I am honored to be on the list of former coaches that includes the names of men like Lou Saban and Chuck Knox, coaches whom I have always held in high esteem. I am so fortunate to have worked with general managers such as Bill Polian and John Butler. They are the best. No, that is not just some convenient tagline, because they *are* the best!

So often overlooked in what contributes to a team's success are the assistant coaches. It has often been my contention that in the NFL there is no such thing as a "good coach." What you must have in order to succeed is a "good coaching staff." Was I lucky, or what?

Football should be fun, and it has been fun for me to participate in writing this book and in working with Jeff Miller and with all the people at Triumph Books. Now, it's time for you to have some fun in reading it. Enjoy.

And, oh yeah, Go Bills! Beat the Dolphins! Beat the Patriots! Beat the Jets! Beat...etc!

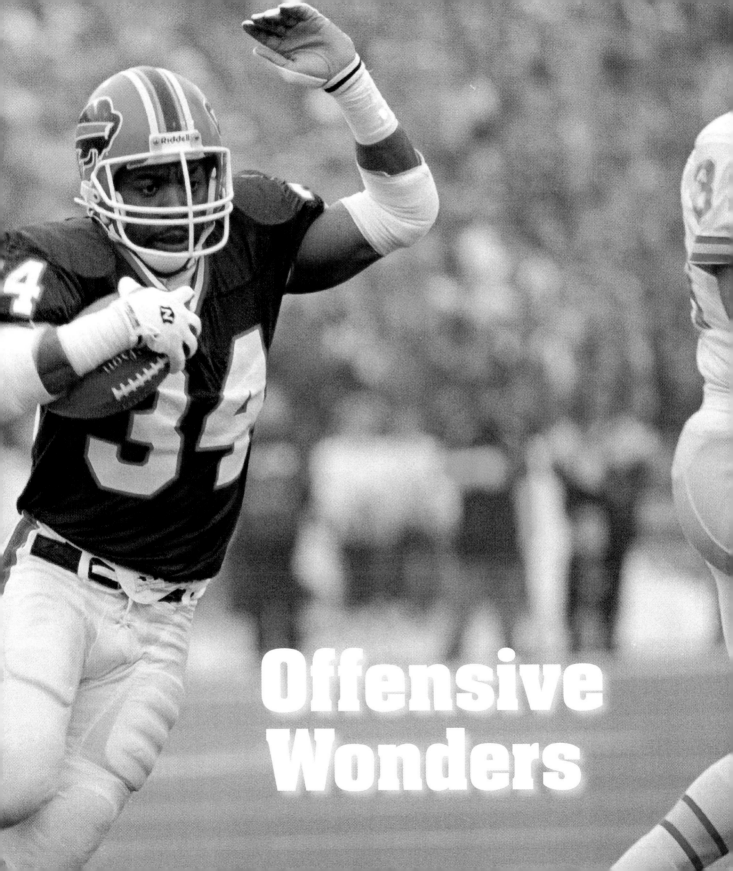

Offensive Wonders

December 16, 1973

Two Grand

Simpson Becomes First Back in History to Exceed 2,000 Yards

O.J. Simpson had already surpassed Jim Brown's single-season rushing record of 1,863 yards earlier that same day, but the man known simply as "Juice" and his Buffalo Bills teammates were now focused on a loftier milestone: 2,000 yards. Brown had established his mark 10 years before, and no other back had even come close to breaking it until Simpson came along. He had led the league in rushing the previous year, amassing 1,251 yards as the Bills began to gel as a unit under the guidance of head coach Lou Saban, who had returned to the fold in 1972 after a six-year absence and made the former No. 1 draft pick the focal point of the offense. Expectations soared as the Bills returned for training camp in 1973, with predictions of a playoff berth and another rushing title for Simpson emanating from the locker room. One player, sophomore guard Reggie McKenzie, wasn't kidding when he confidently predicted that

Simpson—behind Saban's strategic plan and a solid offensive line—could become the first man to break the 2,000-yard barrier.

Now, 2,000 yards in a 14-game season was a tall order—a back would have to average about 143 yards per game to reach that milestone. Brown had averaged only 133 yards per game in his record-setting 1963 campaign. While the rest of the team felt it was attainable, Simpson himself wasn't so sure. "O.J. will be the first to tell you that he didn't think it was possible," McKenzie told author Randy Schultz in 2003. "It wasn't until the seventh game against the Kansas City Chiefs [the midpoint of the season and the game in which Simpson surpassed 1,000 yards] that O.J. believed he could go for 2,000." The season had gone almost according to plan, as Simpson rushed for 1,584

> **I**t hasn't hit me yet, but I guess it will when I get home. It's just so hard to believe.
>
> —BILLS RUNNING BACK O.J. SIMPSON

On December 16, 1973, O.J. Simpson's final carry of the season put him over the 2,000-yard rushing mark. *(Photo courtesy Getty Images)*

yards in the first 12 games—an average of 132 yards per game. He would need to average 140 yards in the remaining two games to surpass Brown's mark. However, it would take 208 yards per game to hit the magic two-century mark. Week 13, played against the New England Patriots on a snow-covered Rich Stadium field, saw Simpson rush for 219 yards, pulling him within 61 yards of Brown's record but 197 shy of 2,000.

The final game of the season pitted the Bills against Joe Namath and the 3–10 New York Jets at Shea Stadium. It was another cold, snowy day that also marked the farewell game for Jets coach Weeb Ewbank, who had announced his retirement after a Hall of Fame career.

Simpson gained 57 yards on Buffalo's first possession, which Jim Braxton capped with a one-yard plunge for a 7–0 lead. On the first play of the Bills' next drive, Simpson surpassed his childhood hero with a six-yard run to the left behind the blocking of rookie guard Joe DeLamielleure. The game was stopped, and referee Bob Frederic presented Simpson with the ball he had lugged for the record. After a short celebration, Simpson, perhaps losing focus on the task at hand, fumbled the ball away in the very next play.

The record now in the books, the Bills focused on realizing the prediction made by Reggie McKenzie back in training camp. It was early in the fourth quarter with the Bills up 31–7 when the offense knew they were close. "Joe Ferguson came in and said I needed 50 yards for 2,000," Simpson said. "We broke 20 off right away, and we were going after it then." At 8:32, Simpson reached the milestone with a seven-yard run through left guard.

According to DeLamielleure, "The play called for O.J. to hit the line behind his roomie McKenzie, who opened a big hole for him." Another celebration ensued, but this time Simpson did not return to the game. With 2,000 yards tucked away and the game well in hand, there was nothing left to prove.

Simpson's final total of 2,003 yards led the NFL, giving Simpson his second consecutive rushing title. The members of Simpson's offensive line (guards McKenzie and DeLamielleure, tackles Donnie Green and Dave Foley, center Mike Montler and tight end Paul Seymour), in recognition for their part in "turning on the Juice," were known forever after as The Electric Company. The event thrust Simpson into the national limelight, and he became arguably the most famous athlete on the planet (aside from Muhammad Ali). It would be another 11 years before Eric Dickerson of the Los Angeles Rams became the second man to reach 2,000 yards and shatter Simpson's record with 2,105 in 1984, by which time the regular season had been expanded to 16 games, making Simpson's accomplishment all the more meaningful. But Bills fans will always remember who did it first.

> **I** told O.J. during the summer, 'Let's shoot for two grand and really set the world on fire,' and we did.
>
> —BILLS GUARD REGGIE MCKENZIE

Game Details

Buffalo Bills 34 • New York Jets 14

Bills	7	14	7	6	**34**
Jets	7	0	0	7	**14**

Date: December 16, 1973
Team Records: Bills 8–5, Jets 4–9
Scoring Plays:
BUF—TD Braxton 1-yard run (Leypoldt PAT)
NY—TD Barkum 48-yard pass from Namath (Howfield PAT)
BUF—TD Simpson 13-yard run (Leypoldt PAT)
BUF—TD Cahill 51-yard punt return (Leypoldt PAT)
BUF—TD Braxton 1-yard run (Leypoldt PAT)
BUF—FG Leypoldt 12 yards
BUF—FG Leypoldt 11 yards
NY—TD Caster 16-yard pass from Namath (Howfield PAT)

O.J. Simpson

O.J. Simpson, who attended the University of Southern California, won the Heisman Trophy as the top college player in the nation in 1968. The Buffalo Bills selected him as the first overall draft pick in 1969, the last year before the actual AFL-NFL merger.

After three disappointing seasons in which he failed to come close to gaining 1,000 yards, Simpson's career took a decided turn in 1972 when Lou Saban took over as head coach. Saban knew he had a serious weapon in Simpson and decided it was time to shoot it. It didn't take long for Saban's strategy to reap rewards, as Simpson paced the NFL with 1,251 yards that same year. It would be Simpson's first of four rushing titles over the next five seasons, which included the historic 2,003-yard effort of 1973. However, most historians rate 1975 as Simpson's best year, when he rushed for 1,817 yards on 329 carries (an average of 5.5 yards) and caught 28 balls for 426 yards. He also set an NFL record by scoring 23 total touchdowns (16 rushing, 7 receiving), breaking the previous mark of 22 held by Gale Sayers.

Simpson capitalized on his fame as an athlete to become a popular television and movie star. In addition to literally hundreds of television appearances (which included commercials, variety shows, prime time dramas, and made-for-TV movies), Simpson appeared in several big screen films, including *The Klansman* (1974), *The Towering Inferno* (1974), *Killer Force* (1976), *The Cassandra Crossing* (1976), *Capricorn One* (1978), and the *Goldie and the Bear* series. But perhaps his best-known role was as Detective Nordberg in the three *Naked Gun* movies. He also appeared in the popular 1977 television miniseries *Roots*. From 1983–85, Simpson was a commentator on ABC's *Monday Night Football*.

O.J. Simpson won his second consecutive rushing title in 1973.

November 22, 1981

Big Ben

Hooks Hauls in Ferguson's Desperation Throw for Buffalo Victory

After going 11–5 in 1980 to claim the AFC East Division crown, the Bills continued their winning ways in 1981, starting the year with a 6–3 record, good for second place in the division behind the Miami Dolphins. But they hit a late-season slump and lost two straight, including an embarrassing 24–0 loss to the lowly St. Louis Cardinals, and the team was in jeopardy of falling out of the playoff picture. Desperate to build some momentum as they headed into the home stretch of the season, it was to Buffalo's good fortune that the hapless New England Patriots were coming to town for this Week 12 meeting at Rich Stadium. The Bills needed someone they could beat up on, and the 2–9 Patriots fit the bill.

Many of the 71,592 paying customers had not yet reached their seats when Nick Mike-Mayer opened the scoring with a 28-yard boot early in the first quarter. New England responded later in the quarter when Andy Johnson hit Stanley Morgan for a 56-yard touchdown pass on a halfback option play, giving the Pats a 7–3 lead. The Bills, despite losing starting halfback Joe Cribbs to an injury, reclaimed the lead in the second on Mike Mayer's 23-yard field goal and an 11-yard pass from Joe Ferguson to Roland Hooks—filling in for Cribbs—making it a 13–7 ball game at the half.

Roland Hooks (25) is congratulated by teammates Joe Devlin (70) and Jim Haslett (55) after scoring the touchdown that secured the last-minute win over the New England Patriots. *(Photo courtesy AP Images)*

The Patriots registered the only points of the third period, a 43-yard John Smith field goal, leaving the Bills with a slim 13–10 lead going into the final frame. Patriots signal-caller Matt Cavanaugh took control of the game late in the quarter, hitting Morgan with a 65-yard strike that put the ball on the Buffalo 5, setting up the go-ahead touchdown toss to tight end Dan Hasselback with 1:56 to play. On the ensuing possession, Ferguson was intercepted by Rick Sanford, and the game appeared to be all but over, sending a throng of fans rushing toward the exits. The Bills used all three timeouts and forced a quick three-and-out series to get the ball back with 35 seconds left, but with no timeouts and the ball resting on their own 27, things looked hopeless. But not to Joe Ferguson. On first down, Ferguson dropped back and fired a strike down the middle of the field to Hooks, who made a spectacular over-the-shoulder grab to move the ball 37 yards to the New England 36. Ferguson then hurried his team into formation and promptly threw the ball out of bounds to stop the clock with 12 seconds to go. Ferguson entered the huddle and called the play the Bills referred to as Big Ben, or more commonly known as a Hail Mary pass, in which a team floods one side of the field with receivers for a desperation throw that they pray will be successfully completed for a touchdown or long gain.

Hooks lined up on the right side of the formation along with wideouts Jerry Butler and Frank Lewis. At the snap, all three sprinted toward the New England end zone, where they were greeted by six Patriot defenders. Ferguson launched the ball toward the corner of the field, and a mass of hands reached up to bat it in one direction or another. Patriots linebacker Mike Hawkins was able to get a good tip but inadvertently directed the ball into Hooks' welcoming arms. The desperate Patriots swarmed in to separate Hooks from the ball, but when he emerged from the pile, the only thing he had lost was his wind. Touchdown!

The Bills had pulled off a stunning come-from-behind win on a desperation play with five seconds left.

"Frank Lewis is the jumper in the middle," Hooks explained. "He tried to bat the ball to either me or Jerry Butler. I just happened to be in the right place at the right time. All I was thinking was, 'Don't drop it.' I couldn't believe it. It was like what was going on wasn't real."

The thrilling victory had the desired effect, putting Buffalo back on the right track that led to a 4–1 record down the stretch, including a Week 13 victory over the Washington Redskins in which Hooks ran for 109 yards and two touchdowns on 19 carries. The strong finish left the Bills with a 10–6 record, good enough for a Wild Card berth in the AFC playoffs, their second straight postseason appearance.

> **L**uck is the residue of design. We had some luck, but a little luck is necessary to be consistent winners in the NFL.
>
> —BILLS HEAD COACH CHUCK KNOX

Game Details

Buffalo Bills 20 • Patriots 17

Patriots	7	0	3	7	**17**
Bills	3	10	0	7	**20**

Date: November 22, 1981

Team Records: Bills 6–5, Patriots 2–9

Scoring Plays:

BUF—FG Mike-Mayer 28 yards

NE—TD Morgan 56-yard pass from Johnson (Smith PAT)

BUF—FG Mike-Mayer 23 yards

BUF—TD Hooks 11-yard pass from Ferguson (Mike-Mayer PAT)

NE—FG Smith 43 yards

NE—TD Hasselback 5-yard pass from Cavanaugh (Smith PAT)

BUF—TD Hooks 36-yard pass from Ferguson (Mike-Mayer PAT)

Roland Hooks

Long-time Bills fans remember Roland Hooks mainly for two things: the last-minute touchdown catch that beat the Patriots in 1981, and his spectacular four-touchdown performance against the Cincinnati Bengals in 1979. For Buffalo coaches, however, Hooks was a super-sub and consummate role player, filling in ably for every Bills back from O.J. Simpson to Joe Cribbs, notching three 100-yard rushing games and the 100-yard receiving game that led to the Bills victory described above.

Hooks came to the Bills in 1975 as a 10th-round draft pick out of North Carolina State. At that time, the Bills had perhaps the greatest running back

who ever lived in Simpson, along with two holdover backups in Don Calhoun and Gary Hayman, so Hooks' odds of making the team were long at best. He was never given a chance to find out after he contracted hepatitis and was forced to sit out the entire season. When he returned for camp in 1976, Calhoun and Hayman were gone, and Hooks made the most of his opportunity, playing well enough to secure the backup spot behind Simpson and becoming a valuable special-teams performer.

When Simpson sustained a season-ending injury midway through the 1977 campaign, Hooks stepped in and played well, carrying the ball 128 times for 497 yards, including a superb performance against the Patriots on November 6 when he rushed 27 times for a very Simpson-esque 155 yards. Hooks' most notable individual outing came on September 9, 1979, when he scored four touchdowns (3, 32, 4, and 28 yards) in just five carries in the Bills 51–24 rout of the Bengals.

In 1981, Hooks enjoyed his best year, turning in 100-yard performances in two consecutive weeks—first compiling 111 yards on six catches against the Pats on November 22, then gaining 109 yards in 19 carries against the Washington Redskins the following week. He also led the team in punt returning that year, bringing back 17 kicks for 142 yards (8.4-yard average).

In his seven seasons with Buffalo, Hooks gained 1,682 yards rushing and 12 touchdowns on 399 attempts (4.2-yard average). He was on the receiving end of 96 passes, which were good for 950 yards and three scores.

Bills running back Roland Hooks had a productive 1981 season.
(Photo courtesy Getty Images/ Takashi Makita/NFL)

O.J. Simpson (32) tries to elude linebacker Jack Ham (59).

September 28, 1975

O.J. Rips Steel Curtain

Simpson's Long Run Caps 228-Yard Performance Against
Pittsburgh's Steel Curtain

The Buffalo Bills had payback on their minds when they traveled to
Pittsburgh in Week 2 of the 1975 season. The previous season had
seen the Bills finish 9–5 to clinch a Wild Card seed for their first
playoff berth since 1966. But what had been a season of revival for
the team came to an inglorious end when they faced the Steelers
in the AFC East Divisional Playoff Game in Pittsburgh and were
treated to a 32–14 schooling at the hands of the future Super Bowl
champions. For the Bills, eager to redeem the devastating loss, the
rematch could not have come soon enough.

"We were there to get revenge because they beat us in 1974," recalled guard Joe
DeLamielleure. "[Offensive line coach Jim] Ringo had this game as a focus point from
the beginning of camp because he wanted to avenge the loss, particularly the way the
Steel Curtain had shut down O.J.'s running game [49 yards on 15 carries]."

Pittsburghers were also eagerly awaiting this game, as evidenced by the fact that
more turned out for the rematch (49,348) than were present for the playoff game the
year before (48,321). After witnessing a scoreless first period, the crowd saw Buffalo
take the game's initial lead early in the second quarter when John Leypoldt made good
from 37 yards out. The Bills extended the lead later in the quarter when defensive end
Earl Edwards picked up Terry Bradshaw's fumble and lateraled to Mike Kadish, the
big defensive tackle who rumbled 26 yards for the touchdown. The stunned Steelers
retired to the locker room down 10–0.

The Bills continued to pour it on in the third, as Joe Ferguson capped a 51-yard drive by hitting tight end Reuben Gant from seven yards out, making it a 17–0 score. Buffalo's inspired defense then forced a Pittsburgh punt, but Bobby Walden's kick rolled out of bounds at the Buffalo 3. No matter, for this was a day when the Bills could do little wrong. On third-and-1 from the 12, Ferguson handed off to Simpson, who started to his right and burst through the line and into the clear. Once fullback Jim Braxton had taken linebacker Jack Ham out of the equation with a key block, Simpson outran the entire Steel Curtain defense—featuring four future Hall of Famers—en route to a sensational 88-yard touchdown run.

"It was our 46 play," Simpson explained. "Joe called something else in the huddle, either a sneak or Braxton straight ahead. They were looking for it, too. Jim made the big block, and soon I realized it was a footrace."

According to DeLamielleure, much of the success of the play had to do with a barely noticeable adjustment in the interior of the Bills offensive line. "One thing that helped was a narrower gap than normal between [center] Mike Montler and me. Usually, it's a foot between us. I cut it down to six inches and [guard] Reggie McKenzie did the same thing on Mike's other side. It worked out exceptionally well." Indeed.

John Leypoldt's failed conversion attempt could not quiet the raucous Buffalo sideline, as the Bills took a commanding 23–0 lead over the defending champs. The Steelers finally broke the goose egg with less than a minute left in the third quarter after a blocked Marv Bateman punt was returned to the Buffalo 6. Franco Harris went over from the 2 shortly thereafter, but the Bills came back on their next possession to seal the deal with a 28-yard scoring pass from Ferguson to Bob Chandler. The Steelers scored two more mop-up touchdowns to make it look respectable, but they were never in it to begin with. The Bills left Steel Town with a convincing 30–21 upset.

Simpson ended the day with 227 yards on 28 carries—the fourth 200-yard game of his career. The Bills improved to 2–0 on the season and appeared to be a team of destiny as they rattled off subsequent victories over the Denver Broncos and Baltimore Colts to mark their first 4–0 start since 1965. However, the club went into a tailspin that began with a last-minute loss to the Giants in Week 5 and lost five of their 10 remaining games, finishing third in the AFC East and missing the playoffs.

We all know what became of the Steelers.

> **I** attribute this showing to Jim Ringo. He's the best line coach in football.
>
> —BILLS GUARD JOE DELAMIELLEURE

Game Details

Buffalo Bills 30 • Pittsburgh Steelers 21

Bills	0	10	13	7	**30**
Steelers	0	0	7	14	**21**

Date: September 28, 1975

Team records: Bills 1–0, Steelers 1–0

Scoring Plays:
BUF—FG Leypoldt 37 yards
BUF—TD Kadish 26-yard fumble return (Leypoldt PAT)
BUF—TD Gant 7-yard pass from Ferguson (Leypoldt PAT)
BUF—TD Simpson 88-yard run (PAT failed)
PIT—TD Harris 2-yard run (Gerela PAT)
BUF—TD Chandler 28-yard pass from Ferguson (Leypoldt PAT)
PIT—TD Grossman 20-yard pass from Gilliam (Gerela PAT)
PIT—TD Harris 1-yard run (Gerela PAT)

Buffalo Bills in the Pro Football Hall of Fame

O.J. Simpson became the first member of the Buffalo Bills family to be enshrined in the Pro Football Hall of Fame when he received that honor in 1985. There are now nine Buffalo Bills in the Hall of Fame:

Joe DeLamielleure – Class of 2003 (Guard, Bills 1973–79, '85; Cleveland Browns 1980–84)

Jim Kelly – Class of 2002 (Quarterback, Bills 1986–96)

Marv Levy – Class of 2001 (Head Coach, Bills 1986–97; Kansas City Chiefs 1978–82)

James Lofton – Class of 2003 (Wide Receiver, Bills 1989–92; Green Bay Packers 1978–86; Los Angeles

Raiders 1987–88; Los Angeles Rams 1993; Philadelphia Eagles 1993)

Billy Shaw – Class of 1999 (Guard, Bills 1961–69)

O.J. Simpson – Class of 1985 (Running Back, Bills 1969–77; San Francisco 49ers 1978–79)

Bruce Smith – Class of 2009 (Defensive End, Bills 1987–99; Washington Redskins 2000–03)

Thurman Thomas – Class of 2007 (Running Back, Bills 1988–99; Miami Dolphins 2000)

Ralph C. Wilson Jr. – Class of 2009 (Owner, 1960–present)

O.J. Simpson (32) and guard Joe DeLamielleure (68) are members of the Pro Football Hall of Fame.

October 11, 1969

Preston Ridle...Who?

Ridlehuber's Halfback Option Pass to Moses Helps Bills Beat Pats

With star rookie running back O.J. Simpson being held out of this contest as a precautionary measure after sustaining a concussion in the previous week's game at Houston, the Bills were forced to press newly signed Preston Ridlehuber into action as the backup for starting halfback Max Anderson. It proved to be one of the most serendipitous moments in the team's brief existence, as Ridlehuber pulled off one of the most memorable plays ever seen at the old Rockpile.

For most of the game, Ridlehuber's involvement was limited to special teams. It seemed the former Oakland Raider would have little bearing on the outcome, as the Bills held a 16–13 lead midway through the fourth quarter. Fullback Wayne Patrick, called upon to carry the brunt of the load in Simpson's absence, was playing superbly (he would finish the game with 131 yards on 17 carries). He had opened the scoring with a two-yard plunge midway through the first quarter. The Patriots came back later in the period when Carl Garrett scored on a one-yard run that was set up by an interception by linebacker Marty Schottenheimer, the former Buffalo

Bill. But the conversion attempt failed, leaving the Bills up by a point. Patrick tore off a 72-yard run midway through the second to set up Bruce Alford's 24-yard field goal, giving Buffalo a 10–6 lead that stood until halftime.

Alford kicked a 22-yarder late in the third quarter to give the Bills a 13–6 advantage, but the Patriots tied it on their next possession when Mike Taliaferro connected with Charley Frazier from 29 yards out, making it 13–13 going into the final frame. Alford and Boston kicker Gino Cappelletti traded field goals early in the fourth quarter to make it a 16–16 game, setting the stage for the dramatic ending. With less than six minutes remaining, the Bills took possession and drove into Boston territory. Max Anderson was forced to leave the game after linebacker John Bramlett knocked out several of his teeth with a vicious tackle.

Enter Mr. Ridlehuber. Wearing No. 31 and not having been with the team long enough to even have a nameplate sewn on to his jersey, Ridlehuber was virtually unknown to all but a handful of the more than 46,000 souls present. With the ball resting at the Boston 45, the right-handed Ridlehuber took James Harris' handoff and rolled left. The Patriot defenders came up to play the run only to see

Running back O.J. Simpson's concussion forced him to the sideline and Preston Ridlehuber became the backup for starting halfback Max Anderson.
(Photo courtesy AP Images)

Ridlehuber—a quarterback at the University of Georgia—slow up, turn his body, and throw a deep floater to receiver Haven Moses, who was standing wide open at the 10-yard line. The defensive back closed quickly, but Moses outran him to the end zone for the go-ahead score with 5:02 left. The defense came through and held off the Patriots the rest of the way, and the Bills escaped with an unforgettable 23–16 triumph.

With the victory, the Bills improved to 2–3 on the season, and this new guy Ridlehuber was the toast of the town. But the happy feeling was short-lived indeed, as the Bills lost their next four games—including a 50–21 drubbing at Oakland the following week—and finished the season 4–10. The fame was fleeting for Ridlehuber as well. Simpson returned to action the next week, and Ridlehuber returned to the bench where he remained for the rest of the year. He never carried the ball again or threw another pass, but for at least one week in 1969—jersey nameplate or not—every football fan in Buffalo knew his name.

Game Details

Buffalo Bills 23 • Boston Patriots 16

Patriots	6	0	7	3	**16**
Bills	7	3	3	10	**23**

Date: October 11, 1969

Team Records: Bills 1–3, Patriots 0–4

Scoring Plays:

BUF—TD Patrick 2-yard run (Alford PAT)

BOS—TD Garrett 1-yard run (PAT failed)

BUF—FG Alford 24 yards

BUF—FG Alford 22 yards

BOS—TD Frazier 29-yard pass from Taliaferro (Cappelletti PAT)

BUF—FG Alford 22 yards

BOS—FG Cappelletti 32 yards

BUF—TD Moses 45-yard pass from Ridlehuber (Alford PAT)

The Legend of No. 31

When Preston Ridlehuber trotted on to War Memorial Stadium turf to face the Boston Patriots on October 11, 1969, bearing the No. 31 on his jersey, he became the first Buffalo Bill ever to wear that particular number in a regular-season game. It was Ridlehuber's first game with the team, and there had not been sufficient time to have a proper jersey with a number and nameplate made, so equipment manager Tony Marchitte gave the reserve halfback the No. 31 until a permanent jersey could be put together. Ridlehuber wore the shirt for just this single game, switching to No. 36 thereafter.

What makes the whole story interesting is the legend behind it. It goes something like this: One of the team's corporate logos from the 1960s featured a football player astride a charging buffalo and wearing a jersey emblazoned with the number 31. According to

Denny Lynch, the Bills long-time archivist, the team had never issued the number before because it was assumed it was reserved for the official team logo. The tradition was broken momentarily when Ridlehuber wore the number in that one game against the Patriots, and the number was placed back into storage where it remained for the next two decades.

"In 1990, I was involved with the number 31 story," Lynch said. "We knew that [first-round draft pick] James Williams wore 31 in college. People kept telling me that 31 could not be used because 'Ralph said so.' I talked to [general manager] Bill Polian, and we asked Ralph, who said, 'I don't know anything about it.' Evidently, the equipment guys had carried on the Tony Marchitte myth that the number couldn't be used. Polian said, 'Give him the number,' and the myth was finally broken."

Preston Ridlehuber

Preston Ridlehuber sure had a flair for the dramatic. Aside from the late heroics of the Buffalo-Boston game of October 11, 1969, Ridlehuber might be best remembered as the hero of the legendary meeting between the Oakland Raiders and New York Jets played the previous November 17. What made the Raiders-Jets game so memorable was not just its spectacular finish but also the furor that resulted when NBC preempted the showing of that finish because the game was running too long and the network had scheduled a children's movie at that time.

Jim Turner's 26-yard field goal had given the Jets a 32–29 lead with 1:05 left in the game. The Raiders were in possession with 50 seconds remaining when the clock struck 7:00 PM Eastern time. Just as Daryle Lamonica—the former Bills quarterback—was getting ready to throw, the network switched to its scheduled running of the movie *Heidi*, a made-for-TV adaptation of the classic story of a young orphan girl growing up in the Swiss Alps. Football fans across the country were mortified, flooding their local television affiliates with calls demanding answers, as well as the final score of the game. Shock appeared to be the common emotion shared by fans when it was discovered that the Raiders had scored two—yes, two!—touchdowns in the final minute to win 43–32. The first score came when Lamonica connected with Charlie Smith for a 43-yard touchdown with 42 seconds left. Jets return man Earl Christy fumbled the Raiders kickoff at his own 12-yard line, and a mad scramble ensued, ending when the ball found its way into the Jets end zone. After clearing the pile of bodies, the officials found Ridlehuber—then a third-string halfback with the Raiders—at the bottom, clutching the ball for the insurance score with 33 seconds to go.

It was not long after that NBC, with CBS following close behind, announced that it would never again interrupt a game until it was over—completely! So

I would have rather had Harris run the play to the other side of the field. This time, I had to run to my left while I sought the receiver. I saw Haven downfield, but I didn't know if I could get the ball to him. I had a little trouble getting into throwing position, but I made it all right. I didn't practice that play at all.

next time you witness a thrilling ending to an NFL game through the warm glow of your television set, remember that some modicum of gratitude is owed to a journeyman halfback named Preston Ridlehuber and his role in the game that will be known forevermore as the Heidi Bowl.

Buffalo Bills wide receiver Haven Moses in 1970. *(Photo courtesy Getty Images/NFL)*

January 6, 1990

The Drop

Kelly's Pass to Ronnie Harmon Falls Incomplete; Bills Lose a Heartbreaker

It was Jim Kelly of the Buffalo Bills against Bernie Kosar of the Cleveland Browns, and the expected fireworks were there for the more than 77,000 fans gathered in Cleveland Stadium as the two teams squared off for the right to play in the AFC Championship Game one week hence.

Throughout most of the game, our Bills were playing catch up. As a result, Kelly wound up throwing 54 passes for a total of 405 yards, including touchdown bombs of 72 yards to Andre Reed and 33 yards to James Lofton. During the course of that roller-coaster afternoon, running back Thurman Thomas racked up 13 catches (two of them for touchdowns) for a total of 150 yards. Despite those imposing numbers, it was another one of the Bills running backs, Ronnie Harmon, upon whom the spotlight would fall as our Bills executed not one but two desperate hurry-up drives during the last 6:39 as we sought to overcome a 34–24 deficit.

Cleveland had taken a 17–14 lead late in the second quarter when Kosar capped off a 55-yard drive by connecting on a three-yard toss to Ron Middleton. It was Kosar's second scoring completion of that quarter. He had teamed up with wide receiver Webster Slaughter for a 52-yard touchdown 10 minutes earlier. That magic combo extended Cleveland's lead to 24–14 early in the third quarter by connecting once again, this time from 44 yards out. On the Browns' next possession, safety Mark Kelso recovered a Kevin Mack fumble at the Cleveland 21. Six plays later, a Kelly-to-Thomas scoring pass cut the margin to 24–21. Our celebration lasted about 10 seconds, because Eric Metcalf took the ensuing kickoff 90 yards for the score, and in

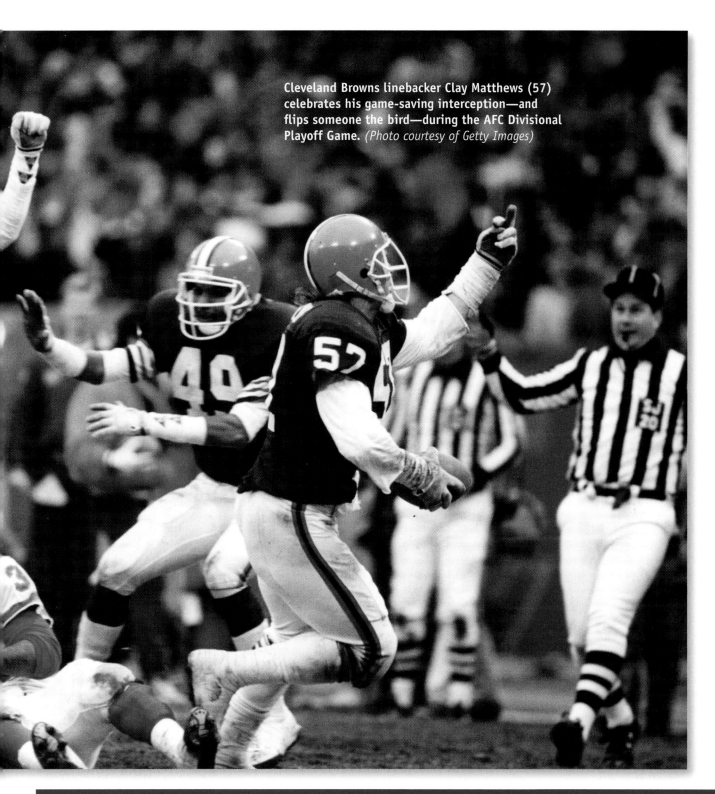

Cleveland Browns linebacker Clay Matthews (57) celebrates his game-saving interception—and flips someone the bird—during the AFC Divisional Playoff Game. *(Photo courtesy of Getty Images)*

the blink of an eye Cleveland was back on top by 10. We weren't about to quit. We took over on our own 20-yard line late in the third quarter. We marched to the Cleveland 12, and on the second play of the fourth quarter, Scott Norwood's field goal narrowed their lead to 31–24.

It was the kind of game in which the Browns knew they couldn't just sit on a one touchdown lead and try to play defense only. They mustered a drive, using a nifty mix of runs and passes that took them from their own 33 to our 29. They took more than eight minutes off of the clock, and their placekicker, Matt Bahr, finished it off by making a 47-yard field goal. It was now Cleveland 34, Buffalo 24.

There were still almost seven minutes left to be played, but I made the decision that we weren't going to dilly-dally until the final two minutes before going into our hurry-up mode.

"Let's go no-huddle—NOW!" I told Jim Kelly. I could almost see the delight on his face as he heard those words. Little did either of us realize at that instant that the Buffalo Bills style for the next several years was about to be previewed. Kelly and his teammates went to work. In the next 2:39, we moved 77 yards to a touchdown. It started with a pass, Kelly to Thurman for 11 yards, then a 15-yard completion to Ronnie Harmon. We were using two running backs and three wide receivers on this drive. Again, Kelly to Thomas for 15, then for five, then for nine. Then it was back to Harmon, this time for a 22-yard completion. Finally, Kelly threw to Thurman for three yards and a touchdown. It was now 34–30. But on the conversion attempt, the ball came out low and struck one of our front-line protectors. It was no good, and we still trailed by four. We would need a touchdown in order to pull it out, and with only 3:48 left

The Birth of the Bills No-Huddle Offense

On the trip back home to Buffalo after the game, Bills offensive coordinator Ted Marchibroda and offensive line coach Tom Bresnahan stopped by my seat on the airplane. They needed to tap me on the shoulder to get my attention since I was deep in thought, mulling over some off-the-wall idea. When I looked up, Bresnahan spoke. "Marv, Ted and I have been talking. What would you think about our making that no-huddle, hurry-up scheme something that we feature right from the opening kickoff next season?" I was stunned—not because of their outlandish suggestion, but because Bresnahan had just echoed the thought that had me so engrossed. And so was born the Buffalo Bills style of offense that would propel us, beginning the following season, to four consecutive AFC championships.

Game Details

Cleveland Browns 34 • Buffalo Bills 30

Bills	7	7	7	9	**30**
Browns	3	14	14	3	**34**

Date: January 6, 1990

Team Records: Bills 9–7; Browns 9–6–1

Scoring Plays:

BUF—TD Reed 72-yard pass from Kelly (Norwood PAT)

CLE—FG Bahr 45 yards

CLE—TD Slaughter 52-yard pass from Kosar (Bahr kick)

BUF—TD Lofton 33-pass from Kelly (Norwood PAT)

CLE—TD Middleton 3-yard pass from Kosar (Bahr kick)

CLE—TD Slaughter 44-yard pass from Kosar (Bahr kick)

BUF—TD Thomas 6-yard pass from Kelly (Norwood PAT)

CLE—TD Metcalf 90-yard kickoff return (Bahr kick)

BUF—FG Norwood 30 yards

CLE—FG Bahr 47 yards

BUF—TD Thomas 3-yard pass from Kelly (PAT failed)

Running back Ronnie Harmon (33) carries the ball. *(Photo courtesy of Getty Images)*

to play, we had to kick off to the Browns and then get the ball back.

We did, and we began our final drive at our own 26 with 2:41 remaining. Fourteen plays later, all passes—four of which went to Ronnie Harmon—we were at the Cleveland 11 with only 14 seconds on the clock. Harmon sprinted out of the backfield, faked a cut toward the middle of the field, then broke out toward the back corner of the end zone. Kelly lofted the ball just over the reach of the man trying to cover Harmon who, while seeking to pull

it in, stole a quick glance down to assure himself that he was getting both feet inbounds. That diversion proved to be just enough to cause the ball to hit his hands a fraction off the mark and bounce to the turf. Incomplete!

One play later, Kelly tried to drill one over the middle to Thomas, but Cleveland's outstanding linebacker, Clay Matthews, intercepted it at the 1-yard line. The game was over. Browns 34, Bills 30. Our season was over, too. It was a quiet locker room after that game.

I saw the same Jim Kelly I've always seen. There's a look of confidence, a look of a man ready to play his game. There wasn't a whole lot to say in the huddle. We knew what we had to do.

—BILLS TACKLE WILL WOLFORD

September 16, 1973

O.J. On His Way

O.J. Simpson Sets NFL Record with 250 Yards in Romp Over Patriots

Reggie McKenzie, the Bills second-year guard, sensed it. He saw his friend and teammate O.J. Simpson come into his own the previous year and win the NFL rushing title. He watched as Lou Saban, the mastermind behind the Bills AFL championships of the 1960s, returned to the fold and developed his offense around the Heisman-winning halfback. He watched as Saban built an offensive line, bringing in McKenzie and fellow guard Joe DeLamielleure, tackle Dave Foley, center Mike Montler, and tight end Paul Seymour to complement holdover tackle Donnie Green and center Bruce Jarvis, which was designed to give Simpson the room he needed to reach the lofty peaks reserved for only the greatest runners in the game. McKenzie was convinced that Simpson was now on the verge of a greatness no other back had ever reached.

"I remember coming to Buffalo that year [1972] and seeing O.J. gain a thousand yards," McKenzie said. "I couldn't believe that my first year with the Bills was his first that he gained over a thousand yards. I knew he could do better—a lot better. I knew as a team that we could do better." But what McKenzie actually meant by better was once thought impossible.

"O.J. said to Reggie, 'I'm going to gain 1,700 yards this season,'" DeLamielleure recalled. McKenzie's reply: "Why not make it an even 2,000?"

O.J. Simpson carries the ball against the New England Patriots on his way to setting an NFL rushing record.
(Photo courtesy AP Images)

And thus a quest was born.

The nature of pro football—or any sport for that matter—is that a season is played one step, or game, at a time. Before McKenzie could say "I told you so" to those who scoffed at his brash prediction, the Bills would have to play 14 games, and Simpson, for his part, would need to average almost 143 yards in each.

Despite a winless preseason, the Bills—mainly because of Simpson's emergence in 1972—were beginning to attract notice from national media, most notably from ABC, which put Buffalo on its popular *Monday Night Football* schedule for the first time ever. It was truly a gesture of respect for a team that many league observers believed was on the verge of regaining its long-lost credibility.

Week 1 found the Bills up in Foxboro, Massachusetts, facing the New England Patriots, and Simpson left little doubt that he was now the top back in the entire league and—if his record-setting performance that day was any indication—among the top backs of all time. Simpson erupted for 250 yards, breaking the old mark of 247 set two years earlier by Willie Ellison of the Los Angeles Rams. The play that set the tone, not only for this remarkable performance but for the rest of the season, came late in the first quarter after the Patriots had taken a 6–0 lead on a Sam Cunningham touchdown run. On the first play of the Bills next possession, Simpson took a handoff from rookie quarterback Joe Ferguson, swept around the right end, slipped through the arms of linebacker Steve Kiner, and broke into the clear along the right sideline.

"I guess their mike [middle linebacker] man hit me," Simpson said. "Then another guy came up and hit me, too. But the second guy knocked me out of the first guy's grasp and gave me impetus. Fortunately, I kept my balance, and then it was just a matter of outrunning everyone."

As Simpson made his way to midfield, a couple more Patriots pursued but no one was going to catch the speedy halfback. He sprinted the rest of the way for a dazzling 80-yard run to daylight, giving the Bills a 7–6 lead from which they never looked back. The Pats managed to keep it close until early in the final quarter when Simpson put

an exclamation point on his brilliant day with a 22-yard touchdown run, giving the Bills a 24–13 lead. Fullback Larry Watkins, who had rushed for 105 yards on the day, closed out the scoring with a 15-yard run, making the final 31–13 Bills.

This was the first of six 200-yard games Simpson went on to record in his illustrious career. In addition to Simpson's individual achievements, the team's 360 combined rushing yards set a Bills standard that stood until 1978. The victory was the first in a Bills season opener since 1967, and it represented the first step toward the team's first winning season since 1966. (The Bills would finish with a 9–5 record.) A return to the playoffs, however, was another year away.

> **H**e'll get [Jim] Brown's record, but 2,000 yards, well, that's a real nice figure.
>
> —BILLS GUARD REGGIE MCKENZIE

Game Details

Buffalo Bills 31 • New England Patriots 13

Bills	7	3	7	14	**31**
Patriots	6	0	7	0	**13**

Date: September 16, 1973

Team Records: Bills 0–0, Patriots 0–0

Scoring Plays:

NE—TD Cunningham 7-yard run (PAT failed)

BUF—TD Simpson 80-yard run (Leypoldt PAT)

BUF—FG Leypoldt 48 yards

BUF—TD Watkins 4-yard run (Leypoldt PAT)

NE—TD Herron 10-yard run (Bell PAT)

BUF—TD Simpson 22-yard run (Leypoldt PAT)

BUF—TD Watkins 15-yard run (Leypoldt PAT)

Joe DeLamielleure

The Bills selected Joe DeLamielleure, an All-American and three-time All-Big Ten guard at Michigan State, with their second of two first-round selections (26th overall) in the 1973 draft. However, a routine physical examination given shortly after the draft indicated that he had a condition that could keep him from realizing his dream of playing pro ball.

"His career with the Bills almost ended before it began," said Eddie Abramoski, the Bills veteran athletic trainer. "When he reported after the draft, we gave him the usual physical, and an abnormality showed up on his EKG."

"When I told [Michigan State head coach] Duffy Daugherty, he was convinced that I was fine to play," DeLamielleure said. "Duffy sent me to see his friend, Dr. Segul, at the Cleveland Clinic. The Cleveland Clinic gave me a clean bill of health. I couldn't get to Buffalo fast enough."

Lou Saban, who had coached DeLamielleure in the Senior Bowl, was equally thrilled. Upon DeLamielleure's arrival at camp, Saban paid the rookie guard the ultimate compliment. "Joe reminds me in so many ways, physically and mentally, of Billy Shaw. And he can be another Billy Shaw." Little could he know that both would one day be enshrined in the Pro Football Hall of Fame.

DeLamielleure impressed throughout the preseason and was rewarded with the starting right guard position for the season opener at New England. He returned that trust with a solid performance that helped his running back make NFL history. "[O.J.] rushed for 250 yards that day, which was an indication of what was to come," DeLamielleure said. "Not every game was going to go that smoothly, of course, but I didn't know that. I thought playing in the NFL was going to be easy."

It wasn't, of course, but along the way, DeLamielleure developed into one of the top guards in the league. He became recognized as the leader of the offensive line that was dubbed The Electric Company for its role in turning on the Juice. DeLamielleure played in five Pro Bowls (1975–79) during his initial seven-year stint in Buffalo. He was also extremely durable, never missing a start in 102 regular-season games during that stretch.

DeLamielleure finished his career with eight All-Pro selections, six Pro-Bowl appearances, and he was voted into the Pro Football Hall of Fame in 2003.

Bills guard Joe DeLamielleure was part of a history-making offensive line. *(Photo courtesy Getty Images/ Tony Tomsic/NFL)*

October 26, 1963

Kemp Comes Through

Kemp Hits Ferguson for Game Winner Against Pats with 28 Seconds Left

In what was undoubtedly the most dramatic last-minute victory in the Bills three-and-a-half-year existence, quarterback Jack Kemp overcame an abysmal series, narrowly evaded the goat tag, and led his team to a 28–21 squeaker over the division-leading Boston Patriots with a sensational 72-yard pass play to wide receiver Charley Ferguson with 28 seconds remaining.

The Bills never should have been in a position to have to win it in such dramatic fashion. In fact, the team at one point held a 21–7 lead on a hat trick of one-yard touchdown runs by Kemp. But the Patriots clawed their way back, tying up things with a 14-point fourth-quarter burst that Babe Parilli capped off with a 77-yard pass play to Art Graham with 5:49 left. On the ensuing possession, the Bills drove to the Boston 11 and were threatening to reclaim the lead only to see the Patriots defense stiffen, sacking Kemp on successive plays and moving the Bills back to the Boston 40.

"People started booing," Kemp said. "The booing was unbelievable. They wouldn't stop booing me even when I was sitting on the sideline. They were mad!"

Coach Lou Saban sent in Mack Yoho to attempt a 47-yard field goal, but his kick fell short and the score remained tied. Fortunately for Kemp, the Bills defense held the Patriots to a three-and-out on their next possession and forced a punt.

"We got the ball back on the 28-yard line," Kemp said. "I'd been throwing slants to Charley Ferguson, which was an 81. I was calling the plays at the line of scrimmage. I would just tell everybody, 'Okay, on the line of scrimmage I'll let you know what to do.' This time we huddled up, and I told them, 'I'm going to call 81, and I want everyone to block just like it's a slant pass,' which means the linemen fire out to keep the opposing linemen's hands down. So I said, 'I'm going to yell 81, and everybody do the same thing as 81, and I guarantee they'll come up and try to stop it, and Charley, you dip behind them and run a post.'"

Kemp was counting on the tendencies of his friend, Boston middle linebacker Nick Buoniconti, whom he knew at times to be over-aggressive. "Buoniconti was one of my best friends off the field. We played against each other with the Chargers and Patriots and the Bills and Patriots, so he knew me and I knew him." Now was the time to exploit that knowledge.

"Now the booing is still going on," Kemp continued, "and it worked perfectly. They blocked, no hands up, I went back three steps and faked a slant to Charley. Buoniconti, the weak-side safety, and the cornerback all converged on Charley. He split by them and went straight for the post. I laid it out, and you could hear the booing turn to cheers as the ball rested in Charley's bosom. It was the weirdest feeling I've ever felt in a football game, because people literally went 'boooyyeeeaahhh!' It was truly classic. He went 72 yards and we won the game, and the goat turns out to be half-hero."

Ferguson, in only his second game with the team since being picked up off the waiver wire from the Minnesota Vikings, was seeing his first extensive action in relief of the injured starter Bill Miller. "Jack read me perfectly, and he had the ball right there," Ferguson said. "Nobody was even

Jack Kemp was known for eluding pursuit. *(Photo courtesy AP Images)*

close to me. After the game, Jack said, 'You know, they had booed me enough. They might have run me out of town. I'm glad you caught that pass!' I said, 'If I'd missed that pass, they might have run us both out of town!'"

The play signaled a change in fortune not only for Kemp and the game but for the entire season, with the Bills improving to 3–4–1. The team would go 4–2 down the stretch and make the playoffs for the first time in its brief history.

> Jack was beautiful. People would try to direct him on the field, and they didn't get anywhere. He directed them right off. Even though he didn't have that way about him that gave you the impression that he was a stud, he really was. He was the general, and everybody knew that.
>
> —BILLS GUARD GEORGE FLINT

Game Details

Buffalo Bills 28 • Boston Patriots 21

Patriots	0	0	7	14	**21**
Bills	0	7	7	14	**28**

Date: October 26, 1963

Team Records: Bills 2–4–1, Patriots 4–3

Scoring Plays:
BUF—TD Kemp 1-yard run (Yoho PAT)
BOS—TD Romeo 6-yard pass from Parilli (Cappelletti PAT)
BUF—TD Kemp 1-yard run (Yoho PAT)
BUF—TD Kemp 1-yard run (Yoho PAT)
BOS—TD Crump 2-yard run (Cappelletti PAT)
BOS—TD Graham 77-yard pass from Parilli (Cappelletti PAT)
BUF—TD Ferguson 72-yard pass from Kemp (Yoho PAT)

Quarterback Jack Kemp joined the Bills in 1962.
(Photo courtesy AP Images)

Jack Kemp

Jack Kemp was a member of the San Diego Chargers until early in the 1962 season, when he was placed on waivers after injuring the middle finger of his throwing hand in a game against the New York Titans. "I threw a pass to Lance Alworth," Kemp explained. "I hit the helmet of a blitzing linebacker and dislocated my right middle finger, but I stayed in the game because I didn't want John Hadl to play. After the game was over, my finger looked like a baseball, so clearly I wasn't going to be able to play. I couldn't even brush my teeth much less throw the ball."

The Chargers placed Kemp on the waiver list on Friday, September 21, 1962, in order to make space for another player for their upcoming game. They planned to recall him after the game, but a paperwork snafu left the quarterback vulnerable to being claimed by other teams. "I got a call from one of the gals in the office that he was put on waivers on Friday," Bills head coach Lou Saban recollected. "I think [Chargers head coach] Sid Gillman was trying to hide him, because if he had gotten through the 48-hour period then he would still have him on his squad. But she called me and said, 'He's going to be available.' He had that bum finger, but I actually saw something in Jack that was special. So I went ahead and claimed him." The Denver Broncos and Boston Patriots also put in claims for Kemp. Despite Gillman's vehement objections, AFL commissioner Joe Foss upheld the Bills claim. The team paid the $100 waiver fee, and Kemp was officially a Buffalo Bill.

"Gillman made a mistake," said Eddie Abramoski, the Bills long-time trainer. "They thought nobody would notice, so we cut a player and played one guy short so we could get him."

"He had a great arm, and he hit the medium passes very beautifully—the 10-yard, 15- or 20-yard out," Saban said. "He could get rid of the ball very quickly, and I felt that could probably save us while we were still in the process of building an offensive line." Kemp would play the rest of his career unable to bend the middle finger on his throwing hand. It seems that when the doctors set the finger, they decided on a utilitarian solution. "They put my hand on a football," he recalled, "and that's how it was shaped. That's the way it is today. It's fused in the shape of a football. I can't bend the middle knuckle."

But the rigid middle finger wasn't the only thing strange about the way Kemp threw a football. Even before the injury, he had an unorthodox method for holding the ball when he passed. "I would put the laces down the middle of my throwing hand," Kemp explained. "I just felt more comfortable putting the laces down beneath the thumb. I felt like I had more balance to the ball. I think I'm the only quarterback—I don't know—but every quarterback I've ever seen used the laces around his middle finger and pinky. I had a very big hand, which stood me in good stead. I used to pride myself that I could throw a football like a baseball, because I was a pitcher in high school and I would wind up and throw it to a receiver as a baseball player would throw a hardball."

Like me, Jack Kemp is an ardent admirer of Winston Churchill. It doesn't surprise me, therefore, that despite the obstacles and even derision that he faced that day that Jack would "never surrender."

It was with great sadness that we learned that Jack passed away on May 2, 2009, after a long battle with cancer. He was 73 years old.

September 13, 1992

Pete Metzelaars, Sprint Champion

Metzelaars' 53-Yard Catch-and-Run Highlights Strange Day as Bills Beat 49ers

What a bevy of renowned receivers there would be on the field when our Buffalo Bills journeyed out to San Francisco to face the high-flying 49ers! Among those luminaries were Jerry Rice of the 49ers plus our James Lofton and Andre Reed—all three of them had Hall of Fame credentials. There were many other fleet-footed wideouts in that game as well, but the man whose performance outshone them all on that pleasant Sunday afternoon in the Bay Area was a big fellow whose speed afoot could at best be described as almost adequate. He was our sterling tight end Pete Metzelaars.

You wouldn't have known this at halftime, however. At that stage of the game, Metzelaars had but one reception. It was for a 20-yard gain, and it did help sustain a drive we were able to top off with

a 41-yard field goal by Steve Christie as the first quarter drew to a close. That allowed us to narrow the 49ers lead to 7–3, since a pass from Steve Young to Odessa Turner earlier in the quarter had resulted in a 23-yard touchdown for San Francisco.

On the series following our field goal, the Young-to-Turner combo continued to plague us. The 49ers started on their own 29, but six plays later, fullback Tom Rathman scored from two yards out to make it 14–3. The key play in their lightning-quick drive had been a 57-yard completion from Young to Turner that advanced the ball all the way to our 5.

The bombs continued to explode throughout the second quarter. After the Niners had taken their 14–3 lead, we answered with a seven-play, 73-yard touchdown march to make it 14–10. Key plays on that trip to the end zone included a Jim Kelly-to-Andre Reed pass for 30 yards, a screen pass to Thurman Thomas for 24 yards, and a 20-yard strike

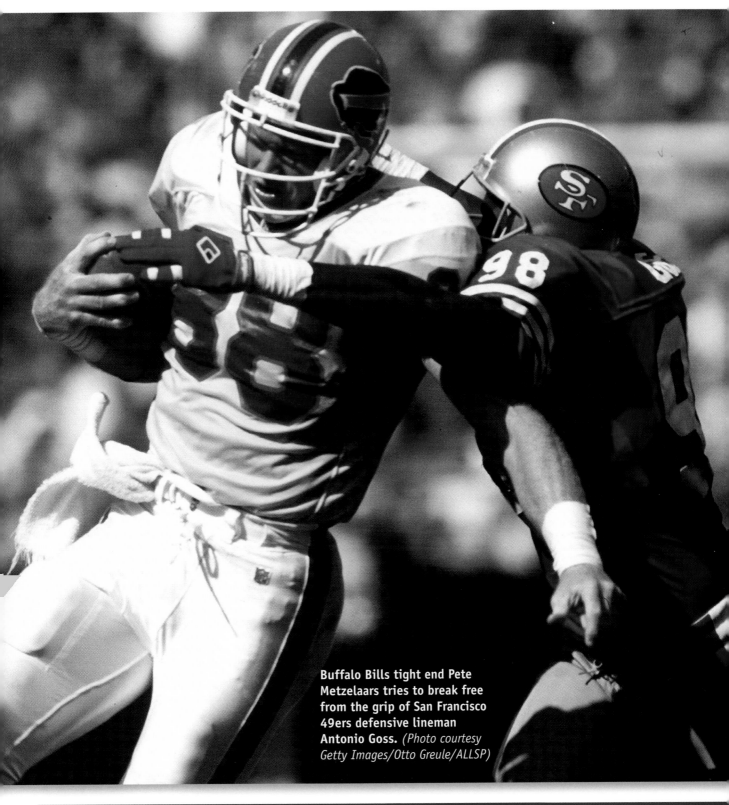

Buffalo Bills tight end Pete Metzelaars tries to break free from the grip of San Francisco 49ers defensive lineman Antonio Goss. *(Photo courtesy Getty Images/Otto Greule/ALLSP)*

Tight end Pete Metzelaars had four catches, 113 yards, and two touchdowns for the day. *(Photo courtesy Getty Images/Rogers Photo Archive)*

into the end zone to Thomas once again. A Mike Cofer field goal upped the 49ers lead to 17–10, but Christie retaliated by kicking a field goal for us, bringing the spread back to four points. Then Young & Co. kept me dizzy by zipping 80 yards in two-minute-drill time to close out the first half. He started out by connecting with wide receiver Mike Sherrard for a 56-yard gain and wrapped it up with a 7-yard toss to another of his wide receivers, John Taylor. At halftime, the 49ers were ahead by a score of 24–13.

During that first half, the 49ers had racked up 328 yards on offense. Steve Young had completed 15-of-21 pass attempts for 257 yards and two scores. He hadn't been sacked, and he hadn't been intercepted, either. Our numbers weren't bad—214 total yards on offense—but they

Game Details

Buffalo Bills 34 • San Francisco 49ers 31

Bills	3	10	14	7	**34**
49ers	7	17	7	0	**31**

Date: September 13, 1992

Team Records: Bills 1–0, 49ers 1–0

Scoring Plays:

SF—TD Turner 23-yard pass from Young (Cofer PAT)
BUF—FG Christie 41 yards
SF—TD Rathman 2-yard run (Cofer PAT)
BUF—TD Thomas 20-yard pass from Kelly (Christie PAT)
SF—FG Cofer 24 yards
BUF—FG Christie 29 yards
SF—TD Taylor 7-yard pass from Young (Cofer PAT)
BUF—TD Metzelaars 53-yard pass from Kelly (Christie PAT)
BUF—TD Metzelaars 24-yard pass from Kelly (Christie PAT)
SF—TD Taylor 54-yard pass from Young (Cofer PAT)
BUF—TD Thomas 11-yard run (Christie PAT)

weren't as startling as those compiled by our opponent. But don't forget, there were still 30 minutes left to play.

We began the second half on our own 20-yard line. Some nifty running by Thomas and a completion to Reed moved it out to our 36. It was from there that Kelly, reading double coverage on both of our wide receivers, found Pete Metzelaars on a go route down the middle. Metzelaars caught it at the San Francisco 39, and there was no bringing him down. He churned his way goalward through all obstacles and accompanied by a chorus of lusty "Go, Pete, Go!" from teammates and coaches who were rollicking along down the sideline. Metzelaars burst into the end zone for a touchdown, and we had again narrowed the gap to four points.

We finally found a way to stymie the 49ers on their next possession. Bruce Smith forced a Keith Henderson fumble, and Cornelius Bennett recovered at our 40. We drove into San Francisco territory, and Kelly hooked up again from their 24 with his newly discovered "deep threat," connecting with "Long Ball" Metzelaars for another score. It was Metzelaars' second touchdown catch within a five-and-a-half minute span. For the first time in the game, eight minutes into the third quarter, we had taken the lead, 27–24.

We returned the fumble favor late in the period, however, and 49ers linebacker Mike Walter recovered at their 40. It appeared as if we would survive that error when Phil Hansen sacked Young, plunging the 49ers into a third-and-20. Unfazed, Young bounced back with a 25-yard strike to John Taylor, who then did a Pete Metzelaars imitation by rambling the rest of the way to a 54-yard touchdown. The quarter ended with the 49ers back in front, 31–27.

Our next possession was foiled by a Merton Hanks interception, but Nate Odomes took it right back by picking off Young at our 28. Twelve plays later, Thomas burst up the middle for an 11-yard touchdown run, and we had recaptured the lead—34–31—with 3:04 remaining. The longest gain on that drive had been a 16-yard completion to—you guessed it—Pete Metzelaars. That catch put

Metzelaars over the 100-yard mark for the day. When it was all over, he had logged four catches for 113 yards and two touchdowns. Pretty darn good for a tight end.

The game was a long way from over. The 49ers began their last desperate drive at their own 20. They got as far as our 29, where they faced a fourth-and-9 with less than a minute to go. Their kicker, Mike Cofer, lined up to attempt a 47-yard field goal. It was wide right.

I guess Scott Norwood was not the only guy ever to go wide right from 47 yards out. But now it was over, and somehow we had won it—Bills 34, 49ers 31.

> You saw two of the finest offensive teams on the field today, and two not very good defensive teams.
>
> —BILLS CORNERBACK NATE ODOMES

The Tight End

Tight end is one of the most unappreciated positions on a football team. The tight end has to be a combination of offensive tackle and wide receiver. He is frequently assigned to block defensive ends or outside linebackers on running plays. In passing situations, if he is not part of the pass pattern, he is often called upon to help out against the opponent's best pass rusher, or he is singly responsible for picking up those blitzing outside linebackers. In short-yardage or goal-line situations, he most often has a key blocking assignment. On the other hand, in many of those short-yardage/goal-line situations where a play-action pass has been called, he is the primary pass receiver. At least he gets some rest when our defense is on the field.

November 18, 1984

One Brief, Shining Moment

Greg Bell's 85-Yard Run on First Offensive Play Stuns Cowboys

The year 1984 was devolving into the worst season the Buffalo Bills had ever endured. The 0–11 record compiled nearly two-thirds of the way through the campaign bested (or is it worsted?) the previous benchmark of 0–10 set back in 1971. The Bills were a team in total disarray as head coach Kay Stephenson struggled to make a contender out of a patchwork of talent, made more ragged by the loss of his three biggest offensive weapons—halfback Joe Cribbs to the USFL, wide receiver Jerry Butler to injury, and wide receiver Frank Lewis to retirement.

Through it all, there was at least one bright spot—rookie running back Greg Bell. Bell was viewed as the heir apparent to Cribbs when the Bills selected him in the first round of that year's draft. After getting off to a slow start in the first four games, in which he carried 27 times for just 77 yards (an average of 2.9), Bell had emerged as the only standout performer on an otherwise pathetic offense, inflating his average to 4.4 over the next seven games by gaining 569 yards on 131 carries. By Week 12, Bell was truly on the verge of breaking out. He sure chose the right time to do it, too, not only by making the play of the game but also by lifting the Bills to their first win of the season during a shocking upset of the perennial powerhouse Dallas Cowboys.

The Bills won the toss and took the game's first possession at their own 15. On the first play from scrimmage, Bell took Joe Ferguson's delayed handoff and ran straight up the middle. He was slowed briefly at the 20 when Dallas safety Michael Downs grabbed hold of his facemask, but Bell managed to break free. Bell then accelerated past the Dallas secondary and into the clear, sprinting untouched the rest of the way for a stunning 85-yard touchdown run, giving the Bills a 7–0 lead just 21 seconds into the action.

"They had lined up in a 6-1 defense," Bell said. "We had seen in films that if we could break the line of scrimmage, only the middle linebacker was there, and after that there was nobody left to make the tackle."

It was a breathtaking play, one that sent the Cowboys reeling. The 'Boys pulled to within four early in the second quarter when Rafael Septien made good on a 40-yard attempt, but that's as close as they would get. The Bills resurgent defense rose to the occasion, as safety Rod Kush

Greg Bell was the only offensive standout for the 1984 Buffalo Bills. *(Photo courtesy Getty Images/George Rose)*

Greg Bell

When the Bills drafted Notre Dame running back Greg Bell in the first round of the 1984 draft, they felt they had secured the man to replace Joe Cribbs, who had left the team to join the Birmingham Stallions of the new USFL. After getting off to a slow start in his freshman campaign, Bell found his legs and went on to become the fourth Bills rookie to record a 1,000-yard season (the others being Cookie Gilchrist, Cribbs, and Terry Miller). In fact, Bell rushed for 1,100 yards and seven touchdowns on 262 carries.

He had another fine season in 1985, augmenting his 883 rushing yards with the 576 he picked up on 58 pass receptions. However, Bell's fortunes went into a downward spiral in 1986 as he suffered through an injury-plagued season in which he appeared in just six games. His injury woes continued into the following year, and many close to the team began to question Bell's toughness and dedication. Some of his harsher critics took to referring to him as Tinker Bell.

"Bell was one of the biggest wastes of talent we ever had," observed Eddie Abramoski, the Bills veteran trainer who taped the ankles of every Bills player between 1960 and 1997. "Bell was a great athlete. His problem was—although he probably wouldn't admit it—he really didn't like football that much, at least not enough to be a full-time professional. It's a tough game when you don't like something."

But Bell made perhaps his greatest contribution to the Bills that year by being part of the blockbuster trade that brought linebacker Cornelius Bennett to the team on October 31. The Bills gave up Bell, their first-round draft choice in 1988, along with their first and second choices in 1989 for the rights to Bennett, who had been holding out after being picked second overall by Indianapolis in the 1987 draft. The Colts then sent Bell and the draft picks they had acquired from Buffalo, along with their own first and second picks in 1988, a second-round pick in '89, and running back Owen Gill to the Los Angeles Rams for superstar halfback Eric Dickerson.

The change of scenery was just what the doctor ordered, as Bell enjoyed the best season of his career, rushing for 1,212 yards and 16 touchdowns in 1988 and being named the league's Comeback Player of the Year. He followed that performance with another solid season in 1989, gaining 1,137 yards and scoring 15 touchdowns, becoming the first back to rush for 1,000 yards and 15 touchdowns in consecutive seasons since Jim Taylor did it for the Green Bay Packers in the 1960s.

Two solid seasons with the Rams notwithstanding, Bell became expendable when the team acquired running back Curt Warner from Seattle, and he was dealt to the Los Angeles Raiders prior to the 1990 season. He saw limited action with the Raiders—who already had Marcus Allen and Bo Jackson on their roster. Bell appeared in just six games that year, his final NFL season.

> We won the game, that's what I'm most happy about. The funny thing is, before the game I told [Bills fullback] Booker Moore that I had a dream that I broke a long run the length of the field for a touchdown on the first play of the game. Booker looked at me and said, 'I had the same dream. Now let's go make it happen.'
>
> —BILLS RUNNING BACK GREG BELL

and cornerback Brian Carpenter each blunted Dallas drives in the quarter with interceptions.

The Bills nursed the four-point bulge until early in the fourth quarter when Ferguson led a 70-yard scoring drive that Bell punctuated with a three-yard touchdown reception, making it 14–3 with 11:48 left. Buffalo's defense, featuring just one All-Pro performer in nose tackle Fred Smerlas, then held off Dallas' constellation of stars the rest of the way to register an unbelievable upset victory.

For the Bills and their fans, it was a brief, shining moment in an otherwise gloomy season that saw the team win just once more to finish 2–14—the first of back-to-back two-win seasons. Bell ended his day with 206 yards on 27 carries and was named the AFC Offensive Player of the Week.

The Cowboys never fully recovered from this embarrassing loss, winning just two more games all year and finishing out of the playoffs with a 9–7 record, marking the first time America's Team had missed the postseason since 1974.

Game Details

Buffalo Bills 14 • Dallas Cowboys 3

Cowboys	0	3	0	0	**3**
Bills	7	0	0	7	**14**

Date: November 18, 1984

Team Records: Bills 0–11, Cowboys 7–4

Scoring Plays:

BUF—TD Bell 85-yard run (Nelson PAT)

DAL—FG Septien 20 yards

BUF—TD Bell 3-yard pass from Ferguson (Nelson PAT)

Running back Greg Bell.
(Photo courtesy Getty Images/George Rose)

Game-Winning Touchdowns

September 10, 1989

Kelly Keeper Squishes Fish

Jim Kelly's Two-Yard Touchdown Run on Game's Final Play Sends Dolphins to Defeat

On a sunny, humid, 88-degree day at Joe Robbie Stadium, our Buffalo Bills ran the ball 27 times for 141 yards. Thurman Thomas gained 94 of those yards on just 13 carries (7.2-yard average). Fullback Jamie Mueller added 18, and running back Ronnie Harmon provided 17 more. Backup fullback Larry Kinnebrew was good for another 10 picked up on his four tough short-yardage situation carries. Even quarterback Jim Kelly carried the ball on one occasion for a gain of a measly two yards, but it was the most important carry of the game and those were the most important two yards in a game that saw the Bills and the Dolphins combine for a game total of 690 yards.

There were a couple of other bizarre circumstances that attended Kelly's two-yard sprint. It came on the last play of the game, and it wasn't even the play he had called as the game clock was winding down while we were trying so desperately to pull out a win in the final seconds of a game that had seemed hopelessly lost just four minutes earlier.

We were trailing 7–3 late in the first half, and we had advanced on a hurry-up two-minute drill drive to the Miami 7. Kelly hit Andre Reed on a quick hitch pass. Reed got to the 5 but was jarred free from the ball. Miami defensive back Rodney Thomas recovered and brought it back to our 45 before James Williams made the touchdown-saving tackle with just 32 seconds left. Dan Marino threw three quick passes, all of which resulted in incompletions, except—uh-oh!—we were flagged for a 34-yard pass interference penalty, putting Pete Stoyanovich in position to kick a 29-yard field goal that boosted Miami's lead to 10–3 at halftime.

Our first series in the third quarter went nowhere, but John Kidd's superb punt pinned the Dolphins back on their own 6. Nate Odomes forced running back Troy Stradford to fumble on first down, and Cornelius Bennett recovered at the Miami 2. Kinnebrew banged it in from there, tying the score at 10 apiece. The next time we punted, it didn't work out nearly as well. Miami's Jim Jensen blocked the kick, and their defensive back, Marc Logan, picked it up and took it in for a touchdown. It was the only punt we ever had blocked during my 12 years as coach of the Bills and darn it, I'm still angry about it.

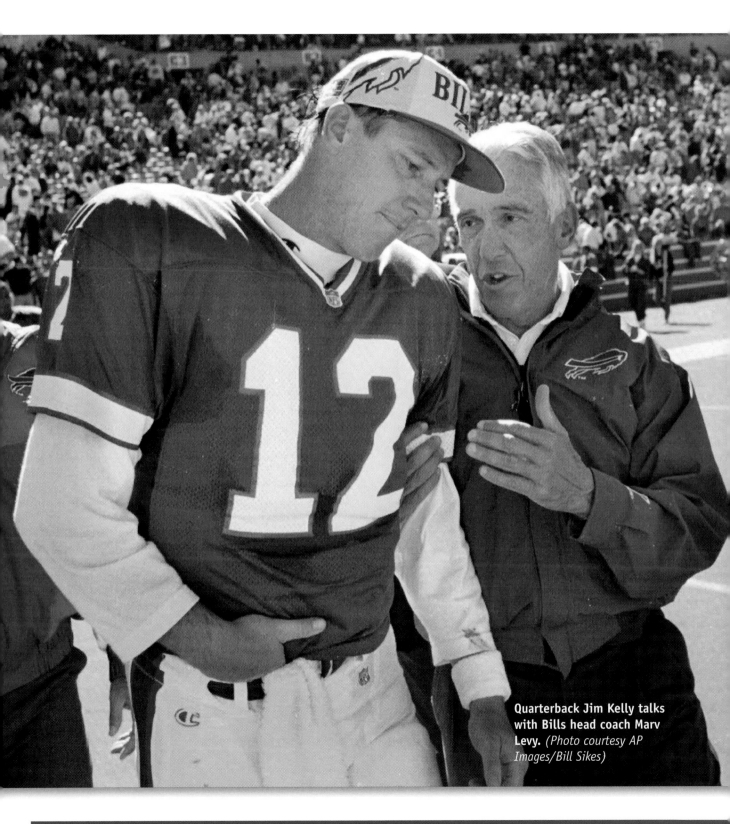

Quarterback Jim Kelly talks with Bills head coach Marv Levy. *(Photo courtesy AP Images/Bill Sikes)*

We retaliated by driving into position for Scott Norwood to boot a 37-yard field goal, leaving us trailing by a score of 17–13 as the fourth quarter began. After a confusing exchange of possessions, linebacker Shane Conlan forced Stradford to fumble, and defensive back Derrick Burroughs recovered for us. We couldn't move the ball, and again we punted. Marino then took over, navigating a time-consuming 14-play drive that led to an eight-yard toss to wide receiver Andre Brown. The score was now 24–13 with only four minutes remaining. Really, the game was over, wasn't it? The logical answer was yes. The actual answer was an emphatic no.

Hurry-up time. In the next 1:20, the Bills sped 82 yards in five plays, the last being a 26-yard scoring pass from Jim Kelly to Flip Johnson. But Miami still had the lead at 24–20. With less than two minutes to go, Miami faced a third-and-10 at their own 39. We were out of time-outs, and if the Dolphins picked up a first down, they could just kneel down and run out the clock. They decided to go for it, and that's when Nate Odomes came through again, picking off his second interception of the quarter to put us back in business at our own 49. Kelly completed five of his next six passes, the final one being a 15-yarder to Andre Reed that got us to the Miami 2. But the clock was still running—eleven, ten, nine, eight…. We rushed to the line of scrimmage and lined up quickly with three wide receivers and just one running back. Kelly called the play. Center Kent Hull snapped it with a mere two seconds showing on the speeding clock.

It was a frantic, last-ditch goal-line pass play with all receivers, along with Thurman Thomas, releasing into the pattern. Kelly had dropped back just two steps when he recognized that Miami's single linebacker had man-to-man coverage on Thurman. When Thurman flared wide to our left, the linebacker had sprinted out to cover him. There was no one backing up the four upfront Miami defenders who were putting the pressure on Kelly. He saw the crease between two of them and decided to go for it. He made it, diving across the goal line an instant before any of Miami's secondary defenders could get there. The game was over. We had won it, 27–24.

None of the Miami defenders were guilty of piling on after Kelly had legitimized the win, but our bench emptied as we all (including me) sprinted down to the end zone to jump in on the celebration. It may have been the hardest Kelly was hit all day, and that included the four times he had been sacked by the Miami pass rushers.

> **O**n that last drive, he was a general out there. There were no doubts in our minds that we were going to make it.
>
> —BILLS GUARD JIM RITCHER

Game Details

Buffalo Bills 27 • Miami Dolphins 24

Bills	3	0	10	14	**27**
Dolphins	0	10	7	7	**24**

Date: September 10, 1989

Team Records: Bills 0–0, Dolphins 0–0

Scoring Plays:

BUF—FG Norwood 34 yards

MIA—TD Stradford 1-yard run (Stoyanovich PAT)

MIA—FG Stoyanovich 29 yards

BUF—TD Kinnebrew 2-yard run (Norwood PAT)

MIA—TD Logan recovered blocked punt in end zone (Stoyanovich PAT)

BUF—FG Norwood 37 yards

MIA—TD A. Brown 8-yard pass from Marino (Stoyanovich PAT)

BUF—TD F. Johnson 26-yard pass from Kelly (Norwood PAT)

BUF—TD Kelly 2-yard run (Norwood PAT)

Jim Kelly

Jim Kelly's qualities as a player, teammate, family man, friend, good citizen, leader, and member of the community are recognized and admired by all who know him. He was also the toughest SOB to ever take a snap from center. But there is one quality often found in a professional football player in which he is somewhat deficient. He is not particularly fleet of foot, and so I recall the agony we all endured as we watched him lower his shoulders and embark upon his land-based journey toward the Dolphins end zone on that glorious day in Miami.

When all the celebration in the locker room had abated after that game, I strode up to Kelly and told him to settle down a bit because an official had called us for delay of game since it had taken him such an inordinate length of time to navigate the few yards needed to get him to his desired destination.

He's still laughing at that one.

The ultimate competitors—quarterbacks Jim Kelly of the Buffalo Bills and Dan Marino of the Miami Dolphins. *(Photo courtesy Getty Images/Al Messerschmidt)*

October 18, 1998

Flutie Boot

Doug Flutie's Keeper Beats Jags

It was a game that pitted student against teacher with Bills quarterback Doug Flutie facing the man who coached him during his Heisman-winning career at Boston College. For the student, facing his former teacher for the first time as a pro quarterback, it was a chance to show just how much he had learned and how far he had come since school let out. For the teacher, who was now facing his former student as head coach of the Jacksonville Jaguars, it was little more than a matter of trying to keep his current team among the ranks of the undefeated.

Jaguars coach Tom Coughlin was the offensive coordinator at Boston College when Flutie gained fame with the memorable Hail Mary pass that won the 1984 Orange Bowl. He knew, maybe better than anyone, that Flutie was as much of a threat with his legs as he was with his arm. But that knowledge didn't prevent Flutie from hoodwinking the entire Jacksonville defense and scoring the game-winning touchdown with less than a minute left and sullying the Jags' perfect record.

Flutie had seen his first significant playing time with the Bills the previous week against the Indianapolis Colts in relief of starting quarterback Rob Johnson, who had been knocked out early in the game with a rib injury. Flutie played superbly, completing 23-of-28 passes for 213 yards and two touchdowns to lead the Bills to a 31–24 triumph. That performance earned Flutie the starting nod against the Jaguars, his first NFL start since October 15, 1989, when he was a member of the New England Patriots.

The Jaguars took the initial lead of the game when Tavian Banks scored on a one-yard run in the first quarter. Flutie tied things up in the second with a 12-yard pass to Eric Moulds, but the Jags went up 16–10 with a pair of Mike Hollis field goals. Steve Christie closed the gap to three points with a 24-yard kick in the third, but Hollis nailed a third field goal to put the Jags back up by six going into the fourth quarter.

With just 1:37 remaining in regulation, the Bills took possession at their own 30 and Flutie led them to the Jacksonville 39. On second-and-6 and 39 seconds left, Flutie found Moulds open along the left sideline and hit him at about the 5. Moulds made an acrobatic catch and fought his way toward the goal line, extending his body to cross the plane with his outstretched hands. The initial call of touchdown was reversed when the back judge ruled that Moulds' knee had hit the turf before the ball crossed the goal line, giving the Bills a first-and-goal at the 1 with no timeouts as the clock continued to run. Flutie spiked the ball to stop the clock with 25 clicks left. On second down, Flutie went back to Moulds in the left corner of the end zone, but the pass was incomplete. On third down, Flutie went to the other side, but his pass to Andre Reed was also incomplete.

It was now fourth-and-goal. The call in the huddle was a Thurman Thomas run to the right, but Flutie audibled at the line of scrimmage, changing the play to a pitch to the left. Thomas, however, missed the audible and ran Flutie's original play. Flutie, after faking a handoff to Antowain Smith, turned to find that Thomas was not where he had hoped he would be. Flutie reacted instinctively, tucking the ball under and scurrying untouched around the left end into the end zone to knot the game at 16 apiece with 13 seconds to go. Christie's conversion gave the Bills the one-point lead and the margin of victory, sending the Jags home with their first defeat and Bills fans home with a renewed hope for the 1998 season.

After the game, Flutie confessed that the bootleg was not by design but rather improvisation. "It was not a naked bootleg," he explained. "It was a pitch to Thurman, but he ran the other play and I ran the pitch for Thurman. He didn't hear the audible, and I just took off."

Quarterback Doug Flutie fires a pass in the second half against the Jaguars. *(Photo courtesy AP Images/Don Heupel)*

Doug Flutie

Doug Flutie was thrust into the national spotlight when he threw the famous last-minute Hail Mary pass that hoisted Boston College to a sensational 47–41 victory over the Miami Hurricanes in the 1984 Orange Bowl. Despite Flutie winning the Heisman Trophy as the top college player that year, NFL teams had concerns over Flutie's height (he was listed at 5'10"), and as a result he languished until the 11th round of the draft (Los Angeles Rams). Determined to prove he should be a starter, Flutie signed with the New Jersey Generals of the USFL and led the team in passing in his one and only season (1985) before the league folded. He returned to the NFL in 1986 and endured brief stints with the Chicago Bears and New England Patriots, who unceremoniously released the Natick, Massachusetts, native after the 1990 season.

Undaunted, Flutie signed with the British Columbia Lions of the CFL, where he was united with his brother Darren, a wide receiver for the team. Over the next eight seasons, Flutie forged a career that some consider the greatest in the history of the league as he won a record six Most Outstanding Player awards (1991–94, 1996–97). Flutie's teams won three Grey Cups (the CFL equivalent of the NFL's Super Bowl), and he was named Most Valuable Player in each of those wins (1992 with the Calgary Stampeders, and 1996 and '97 with the Toronto Argonauts).

Flutie returned to the NFL in 1998 after signing a free-agent contract with the Buffalo Bills. He rewarded the Bills faith by earning Pro Bowl honors after his first season, in which he completed 264-of-354 passes for 2,711 yards and 20 touchdowns (while throwing 11 interceptions) and led them to the playoffs. However, a 24–17 loss at Miami brought an abrupt end to an otherwise terrific campaign. He became a fan favorite for his feats of derring-do and his uncanny knack for eluding pass rushers and scrambling for first downs. By sheer force of will, Flutie was able to overcome the perceived height disadvantage and befuddle defenses stacked against him. To the Buffalo faithful, who saw the diminutive signal-caller as the very reflection of the city's hard-working, blue-collar image, Flutie was the long-sought answer to the quarterback quandary that had plagued the team since Jim Kelly retired.

However, a quarterback controversy developed as coach Wade Phillips flip-flopped between Flutie and Rob Johnson. It came to a head in 1999 when, after Flutie again led the team to the playoffs, Johnson was given the start in the AFC Wild Card Game against the Tennessee Titans. Although Johnson played well enough to win, the Bills lost on a desperation play that has come to be known as the Music City Miracle.

Johnson was given the starting job in 2000, causing more uproar as Flutie fans called radio talk shows and wrote letters demanding that their man be the starter. The complaints appeared justified as the Bills failed to make the playoffs that year. Flutie became an unrestricted free agent in 2001 and signed with the San Diego Chargers, where he played four years before returning to New England in 2005 to play one last season for the Patriots. He played sparingly as the backup to Tom Brady but made history in the season finale against Miami by becoming the first player since 1941 to successfully execute a drop kick in a regular-season game. The play turned out to be the last in a legendary career, as Flutie announced his retirement in May 2006.

Doug Flutie's mobility won the day for the Bills. *(Photo courtesy Getty Images/NFL)*

The teacher had no time to revel in the heroic performance of his former student. He was more concerned about the inexcusable breakdown of his defense, which should have known Flutie might pull off something like this. "Everyone in the ballpark knows that it's a naked bootleg," Coughlin said, still believing that Flutie's run was a designed call. "We had an idea what would be coming. They just did what they had to do at the end and we didn't. It was a bad way to lose."

Coughlin wouldn't be the last coach to feel that way, as Flutie held on to the starting job and led the Bills to a 7–3 record down the stretch, taking them to the AFC Wild Card Game and winning the NFL's Comeback Player of the Year award.

> **B**ig players make big plays.
> —BILLS HEAD COACH WADE PHILLIPS

Game Details

Buffalo Bills 17 • Jacksonville Jaguars 16

Jaguars	7	3	6	0	**16**
Bills	0	7	3	7	**17**

Date: October 18, 1998

Team Records: Bills 2–3, Jaguars 5–0

Scoring Plays:

JAX—TD Banks 1-yard run (Hollis PAT)

BUF—TD Moulds 12-yard pass from Flutie (Christie PAT)

JAX—FG Hollis 35 yards

JAX—FG Hollis 23 yards

BUF—FG Christie 24 yards

JAX—FG Hollis 27 yards

BUF—TD Flutie 1-yard run (Christie PAT)

September 16, 1974

Monday Night Magic

Ferguson and Rashad Lead Bills to Monday Night Upset of Raiders

In front of a national audience on *Monday Night Football*, the Buffalo Bills pulled off one of the most dramatic regular-season wins in club history. Twice in the game's last two minutes, quarterback Joe Ferguson hit Ahmad Rashad for touchdowns—the second one for the victory with just 26 seconds left to play. What makes the win all the more impressive is that they did it without star running back O.J. Simpson, who sat out the second half with a sprained ankle.

The Oakland Raiders were a physical, intimidating team that came into Orchard Park for this season opener basking in the glow of nine consecutive winning seasons. The Bills, on the other hand, were coming off their first winning campaign in six years, having finished 1973 with a 9–5 record that, despite being a five-game improvement over the previous season, was not quite good enough to earn them a spot in the postseason. "The Playoffs!" became the Buffalo Bills battle cry in '74.

The excitement of playing before a national audience on ABC's Monday night showcase was quieted by a rather dull first quarter, which ended in a scoreless tie. The Bills broke the stalemate early in the second stanza when Joe Ferguson connected with J.D. Hill for a four-yard touchdown pass. The Raiders finally broke through in the half's waning moments with a 34-yard field goal from George Blanda. Rather than allowing the clock to run out on the ensuing possession, Bills coach Lou Saban opted to try for another score before intermission. The gamble backfired,

> **N**othing was said in the huddle. We knew we could get back into it. In that situation, I think I can get open any time. Joe was right on the money both times. No way I wasn't going to catch them. I'm emotionally drained.
>
> —BILLS WIDE RECEIVER AHMAD RASHAD

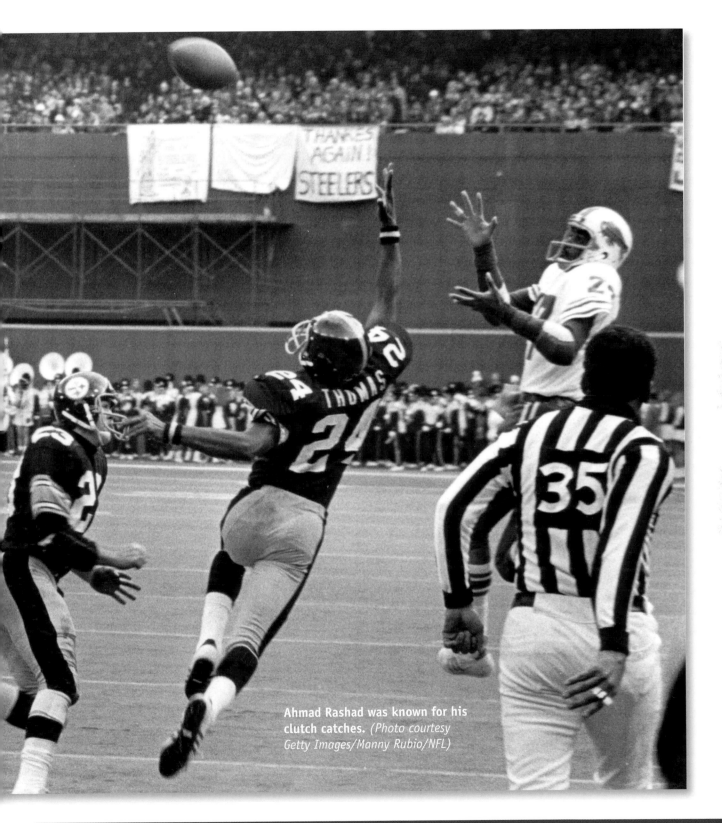

Ahmad Rashad was known for his clutch catches. *(Photo courtesy Getty Images/Manny Rubio/NFL)*

however, as O.J. Simpson sustained a sprained right ankle with 48 seconds remaining while fighting for extra yardage. They settled for a John Leypoldt field goal attempt, but his 47-yard kick sailed wide and the half closed with the Bills ahead by four.

The Raiders seized control in the third quarter, building a 13–7 lead on a 15-yard touchdown run by Clarence Davis and a second Blanda field goal. They held fast to that lead and appeared to have the game well in hand until late into the final frame when Ferguson hit wide receiver Ahmad Rashad—who had beaten defensive back Skip Thomas on a short slant to the post—for a diving touchdown grab from eight yards out to give the Bills a one-point lead with just 1:56 remaining. Buffalo's defense then showed its pluck, forcing the Raiders to punt on their next possession, and the sell-out Rich Stadium crowd sensed its team was on the way to an upset win. But when fullback Jim Braxton fumbled on first down, Raiders defensive tackle Art Thoms recovered at the Buffalo 29 and rumbled in for the go-ahead score with 1:15 to go.

The Bills refused to give up. Taking his place behind center with his team in possession at its own 28-yard line, the man they called the Arkansas Rifle went to work. Ferguson hit Braxton for a 10-yard gain, which turned into a 25-yard advance after Raiders defensive end Horace Jones was charged with roughing the Bills quarterback after the throw. Ferguson then hit Rashad for 20 and Hill for 10, bringing his team to the Raiders 17. A four-yard pass-interference call against Skip Thomas gave the Bills a first-and-10 at the 13. Ferguson's first-down pass to Hill fell incomplete. On second down, Rashad put a spin move on Willie Brown that left the Raiders All-Pro cornerback flat-footed. Ferguson fired a perfect throw that Rashad cradled to his bosom. Touchdown! Leypoldt's extra point gave the Bills a 21–20 lead with 26 seconds left.

But the Raiders fought back and were threatening to pull it out after Ken Stabler passes to Cliff Branch and Charlie Smith brought the ball to the Buffalo 43 with six seconds on the clock. Blanda was sent onto the field to attempt a game-winning field goal, but at this point in his

illustrious career—in his 25th pro season and one day shy of his 47th birthday—50 yards was well out of his range. His kick fell short and wide of the post, and the stadium exploded into a frenzy.

The victory was the Bills second in as many appearances on *Monday Night Football*. It set the tone for a successful season that saw the team finish with a second straight 9–5 record for their first playoff appearance since the 1966 AFL Title Game.

> **O**n that last drive, we knew Joe could take us in if we kept everybody off him. We just had our tails nailed to the ground. Oakland is always physical and they try to intimidate you—get you to worry about your health.
> —BILLS CENTER MIKE MONTLER

Game Details

Buffalo Bills 21 • Oakland 20

Raiders	0	3	10	7	**20**
Bills	0	7	0	14	**21**

Date: September 16, 1974

Team Records: Bills 0–0, Raiders 0–0

Scoring Plays:
BUF—TD Hill 4-yard pass from Ferguson (Leypoldt PAT)
OAK—FG Blanda 34 yards
OAK—TD Davis 15-yard run (Blanda PAT)
OAK—FG Blanda 41 yards
BUF—TD Rashad 8-yard pass from Ferguson (Leypoldt PAT)
OAK—TD Thoms 29-yard fumble return (Blanda PAT)
BUF—TD Rashad 13-yard pass from Ferguson (Leypoldt PAT)

Ahmad Rashad

Ahmad Rashad had only one active season with the Buffalo Bills—1974—but he made the most of it by leading the team in receptions with 36 and playing an integral role in the team's playoff run that year.

Rashad, who was born Robert Earl Moore and attended the University of Oregon, was the number-one draft choice of the St. Louis Cardinals in 1972. It was around this time that he converted to Islam and changed his name to Ahmad Rashad, meaning "Admirable One Led to Truth." A two-time All-America selection at University of Oregon, Rashad is the only player in Pac 10 history to lead the conference in scoring from two different positions (running back and wide receiver).

After two fine seasons in St. Louis, in which he was selected to UPI's All-Rookie Team in 1972 and set an NFL record for the longest nonscoring completion with a 98-yard reception from Jim Hart in a game against the Los Angeles Rams, Rashad was dealt to the Bills for quarterback Dennis Shaw. The speedy, sure-handed wideout won instant fan approval with his two-touchdown performance in the season opener against the Raiders. He turned in his best game statistically on November 3 in the Bills 29–28 win over the Patriots, catching eight balls for 115 yards and a touchdown.

Unfortunately for Rashad and the Bills, a knee injury suffered in an exhibition game against Kansas City caused the budding star to miss the entire 1975 season. He later became embroiled in a contract dispute that led to his departure from the team in 1976, when he signed with the Seattle Seahawks, one of the two expansion teams entering the league that year. His time in Seattle was brief as well, as he was traded to the Minnesota Vikings after just two preseason games. It was during his time with Minnesota that Rashad's career flourished, with four Pro Bowl appearances (1979–82) and a Super Bowl (XI) in seven years. He retired after the 1982 season.

Rashad made a seamless transition from the playing field to the broadcast booth, beginning in 1983 by covering the NFL and other sporting events for NBC. In 1990, he became the host of NBC's *NBA Inside Stuff*. The show later moved over to ABC and evolved into *NBA Access with Ahmad Rashad*. He has won six Emmy Awards for his television work, including one for writing in 1988. He is also the author of *Rashad: Vikes, Mikes and Something on the Backside*.

Rashad was inducted into the National College Football Foundation Hall of Fame in 2007 and is a member of the Minnesota Vikings 40th Anniversary Team.

Wide receiver Ahmad Rashad.
(Photo courtesy Getty Images/NFL)

October 15, 1989

Reich Ready for Prime Time

Frank Reich Leads Dramatic Comeback Win in First NFL Start

The Bills had gotten off to a fast start in 1989, compiling a 3–1 record before being embarrassed by the Colts in a 37–14 drubbing in Week 5. But the score wasn't the worst result of the Colts game. During that debacle, Jim Kelly had been injured, and he wouldn't be ready to play when we took the field to host the undefeated Los Angeles Rams in Week 6. In his stead, Frank Reich—our veteran backup—would be called upon to make his first NFL start. It was Reich's fifth year with the team, and during that span he had thrown a paltry 20 regular-season passes, none of them coming since the conclusion of the 1986 campaign two-and-a-half years before.

If our fans were apprehensive about that circumstance, their concerns were not allayed when on our very first possession, Rams cornerback Jerry Gray picked off Reich's second pass attempt and returned it to our 46-yard line. Bruce Smith sacked Jim Everett and forced the Rams to punt, but returner Mickey Sutton fumbled his fair-catch attempt and the Rams recovered at our 16-yard line. Five plays later, Everett completed a three-yard scoring toss to

fullback Buford McGee, and the Rams led 7–0. The way we continued to play on offense following their touchdown made it seem as if that solitary score would be enough to carry the day. When the first half ended, we had registered just three first downs, and Reich had completed just five of his 15 passes for only 33 yards. Our halftime total yardage was an unimpressive 100, and that came mostly because of Thurman Thomas' 10 carries for 63 yards.

With about five minutes remaining in the second quarter, it was still 7–0. At that point Jeff Wright recovered a fumble by Greg Bell, but we couldn't get anything going and had to settle for a 38-yard field goal from Scott Norwood. Our defense stuffed the Rams on their next possession, and when they punted, Sutton made up for his earlier muff by returning it into Los Angeles territory. With time running out in the half, we put together our longest drive of the day so far—20 yards, baby!—and although it petered out, a second Norwood field goal reduced the Rams lead to one point at 7–6.

The scene didn't change much in the third quarter. With less than three minutes remaining in that period, we had added just one more first down and no more points. The Rams had done slightly better, and when kicker Mike

Lansford made good from 34 yards out, they were ahead 10–6 as we entered the final frame.

That's when Reich began to find his groove. On a drive that began at our own 25, we moved the ball as far as the Rams 23. On the way, Reich completed key passes of 9 yards each to Andre Reed and Keith McKeller. On a crucial third-and-10 situation at our own 36, Reich connected with Thurman for a 13-yard gain. We couldn't take it all the way, however, so we settled for Scott's third field goal of the day. We had pulled to within a point.

That didn't last very long. The Rams came right back with another Lansford field goal and made it 13–9. They pinned us back on our own 14 on the ensuing kickoff, but so what? Reich was hot now. On first down, he teamed up with Andre Reed for a 45-yard gain. Eight plays later we had a third-and-goal at the Rams 1. Reich faked a run to fullback Larry Kinnebrew and then flipped a pass to Thomas in the flat for the touchdown. With 2:13 to go, we had taken our first lead of the contest.

Our defense then forced a three-and-out, and we took over with 1:53 remaining. We had it wrapped up now, hadn't we? All we had to do was protect the ball and run out the clock. But then Thurman Thomas—who just a moment ago had caught the "winning touchdown"—fumbled the ball and the Rams recovered. On the first play, Everett hit wide receiver

Quarterback Frank Reich drops back to pass.
(Photo courtesy Getty Images/Rick Stewart)

Willie Anderson at the Los Angeles 45, and Anderson raced all the way to their go-ahead touchdown.

Our great comeback effort had been thwarted. We had blown it. Oh, yeah? Don't tell that to Frank Reich and the Buffalo Bills. Trailing 20–16 with just 1:17 left, we began our last desperate effort from our own 36. Seven plays later, we were at the Rams 8-yard line. Now only 20 seconds were left to be played. The drive had been kept alive when Thomas (that guy again?), on a third-and-6 situation, turned a dump-off reception into a 17-yard gain.

On the next play, Reich found Reed (that guy again?) in the end zone. Reich threw it, and Reed caught it. The Bills had done it! Final score—Bills 23, Rams 20.

As I frequently told our players, "What it takes to win is simple, but it isn't easy."

Game Details

Buffalo Bills 23 • Los Angeles Rams 20

Rams	7	0	3	10	**20**
Bills	0	6	0	17	**23**

Date: October 15, 1989

Team Records: Bills 3–2, Rams 5–0

Scoring Plays:

LA—TD McGee 3-yard pass from Everett (Lansford PAT)

BUF—FG Norwood 38 yards

BUF—FG Norwood 47 yards

LA—FG Lansford 34 yards

BUF—FG Norwood 40 yards

LA—FG Lansford 36 yards

BUF—TD Thomas 1-yard run (Norwood PAT)

LA—TD Anderson 78-yard pass from Everett (Lansford PAT)

BUF—TD Reed 8-yard pass from Reich (Norwood PAT)

Kent Hull

The man who occupied the pivot position in the offensive line during the Bills' Super Bowl years was Kent Hull. Kent was drafted by USFL New Jersey Generals in 1983 and became an All-Star performer for them over the next three seasons. He came to the Bills on the same day (August 18, 1986) the team signed that other, somewhat better-known USFL refugee, Jim Kelly. Hull became the driving force in our front line for the next 11 years, earning recognition as one of the premier centers in the league, as evidenced by his numerous All-Pro selections and three Pro Bowl appearances. The responsibility of seeing that our difficult-to-run-but-vaunted-no-huddle offense ran smoothly rested just as heavily upon the physical and mental abilities of Kent Hull as it did upon those of our quarterbacks.

Frank Reich

There may have been no better "backup" quarterback in the history of the NFL than Frank Reich. It was amazing how thoroughly he always prepared even though he was aware that, in most instances, it was unlikely that he would hit the playing field on game day. The collaboration and friendship that existed between Reich and Jim Kelly were unique. They each helped to make the other man better and became what I felt was the best one-two quarterback combination in the league. Reich was so well prepared and he practiced in such a studied and dedicated fashion that he was always ready when called upon to enter

> I never really doubted we were going to win the game. We had a few problems early in the game; it took me a while to get going. I just said to myself, 'Frank, hang in there.'
>
> —BILLS QUARTERBACK FRANK REICH

the game with great confidence. That confidence was transmitted to his teammates so that they, too, felt great confidence in how the team would fare if this super-sub was sent into the fray.

Left to right: head coach Marv Levy and quarterback Frank Reich. *(Photo courtesy Getty Images/Andrew Itkoff/AFP)*

October 21, 1990

Kelly-Mueller Connection Caps Another Comeback

Kelly Leads Late Rally to Pull Victory from Jaws of Defeat

Our 1989 season had ended in the AFC Divisional Playoff Game at Cleveland. A dropped pass in the final seconds of our attempt to rally from what had been a two-touchdown fourth-quarter deficit sealed our loss. We now came into Week 6 of the 1990 season sporting a 4–1 record. But in the two games prior to this matchup against the New York Jets, we had to rescue both victories by executing exciting fourth-quarter comebacks. If we were going to win this one, we'd have to do it one more time, because with just 2:38 remaining in the fourth quarter, Pat Leahy's 25-yard field goal had given the Jets a 27–24 lead.

Throughout most of this game, we had been playing catchup. At no time during the contest had we held the advantage. New York, by virtue of an early first-quarter touchdown, had taken a 7–0 lead when running back Freeman McNeil capped a 63-yard drive with a run from

five yards out. The Jets' only pass attempt on the drive was the one that started it off, a 25-yarder from Ken O'Brien to wide receiver Al Toon. On the first play after the ensuing kickoff, Jets defensive tackle Dennis Byrd sacked Jim Kelly for a 14-yard loss at our 21. On the next play, Kelly was intercepted by Erik McMillan, giving New York possession at our 30. But what made the situation even more bleak was that Thurman Thomas, in tackling McMillan, was injured and had to leave the field. Nine plays later, the Jets were in our end zone again and now led 14–0.

We were used to bouncing back, and that's just what we did. We received the next kick and began to march from our own 36. There were two plays that were prominent in the eight-play, 64-yard drive that led to our first points of the game. The first, of course, was the 19-yard touchdown pass from Kelly to Andre Reed at the end of it. The other memorable play came on a second-and-long situation at our own 48. Kelly dropped back to pass, but with no one open, he was forced into a scramble. He ran to his right, stopped, and ducked, then he started back to the left for just three steps before deciding to go back to his right. Thirty yards downfield at the Jets 22, fullback Jamie Mueller was mirroring Kelly's every change of direction. Kelly spotted Mueller and drilled the ball to him. Mueller caught it there for a first down. He'd better!

Let me explain. At our team meeting before practice every Saturday, I would lecture our team about some type of special situation that might come up in a game. Then at practice, we would hold a drill that focused on that particular unusual circumstance. The day before the Jets

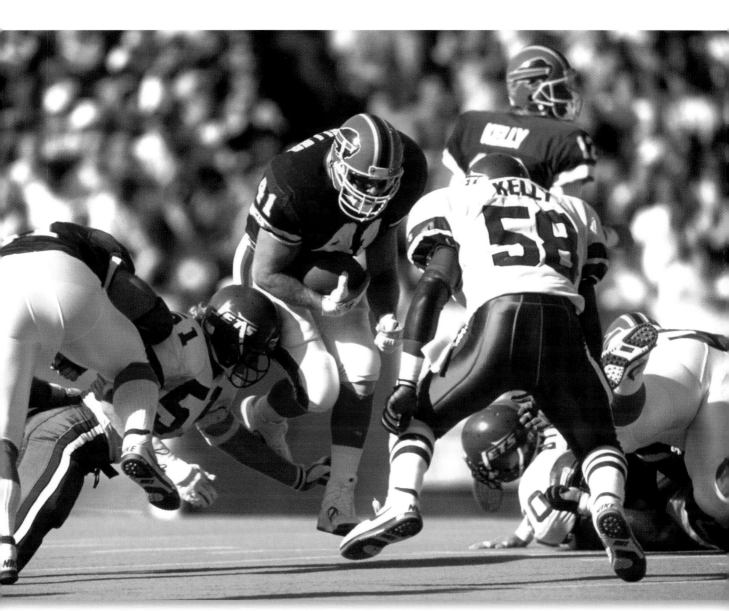

Buffalo Bills fullback Jamie Mueller (41) prepares for a collision with New York Jets linebacker Joe Kelly (58) during the Bills' 30–27 win at Rich Stadium. *(Photo courtesy Getty Images/Rick Stewart/Allsport)*

game, the subject was, "What do we do and how do we do it when our quarterback is forced into a scramble." After the meeting that Saturday, we went to the field and practiced our scramble drill, and although all the receivers were reacting to Kelly's changes of direction, Kelly threw the ball at Jamie Mueller…and Mueller dropped it!

But that was yesterday. For the time being at least, we had narrowed the Jets lead to 14–7. They came right back at us, marching 71 yards to go back in front, 21–7. They were hot, but so were Kelly, Reed & Co. Kelly hit Reed for a gain of 16. Then Kelly connected on a 25-yarder to James Lofton. Now it was Reed on a reverse for a 26-yard gain, and then Kelly to Reed for 14 yards and a touchdown. It was now 21–14, and even though Scott Norwood made a 29-yard field goal one series later just as the half was ending, we went to the locker room trailing just 21–17.

The Jets boosted their lead back up to seven points on their first possession of the third quarter when Leahy made good on a 28-yarder. They then had us pinned back on our own 9-yard line when we incurred a holding penalty on the kickoff return. Not to worry, though. Kelly to Reed for 12 yards. Kelly to Reed for 19 yards. Double coverage on Reed? Okay then, Kelly to Lofton for 60 yards and a touchdown. It was 24–24, and we were in the fourth quarter. That's when the Jets recaptured the lead, 27–24, on Leahy's 25-yard field goal with just 2:38 on the clock.

We began our last drive from our own 29. Two completions to Reed and two more to tight end Pete Metzelaars brought us to a second-and-10 at the Jets 14, but there were only 27 seconds left to play and we were out of timeouts. The Jets came on a blitz that Kelly somehow managed to escape, and into scramble mode we went. Back and forth, back and forth. The clock was winding down fast toward 10 seconds. "Get rid of it, Jim!" I yelled.

He didn't hear me, but he got rid of it anyway. He zipped the ball right at—oh no, not the guy that dropped the ball in practice yesterday. But Mueller, in the end zone, cradled it to his chest and went to the ground. Touchdown! The conversion was missed, but with 12 seconds left we

had taken our first lead of the day. Great kickoff coverage and tackling by special teams star Mark Pike kept the Jets deep in their own territory, and the game ended one play later. Bills 30, Jets 27.

> **T**his is the last thing I ever expected. But when you get the opportunity, you have to make the best of it. I'm blocking weak side and looking for one of the linebackers to come. They both dropped off, so I just find an open area so if Jim needs help or is in a scramble, I try to get in the open field so he can throw to me. And that's what he did.
>
> **—BILLS FULLBACK JAMIE MUELLER**

Game Details

Buffalo Bills 30 • New York Jets 27

Jets	7	14	3	3	**27**
Bills	0	17	7	6	**30**

Date: October 21, 1990

Team Records: Bills 4–1, Jets 2–4

Scoring Plays:

NY—TD McNeil 5-yard run (Leahy PAT)

NY—TD Boyer 1-yard pass from O'Brien (Leahy PAT)

BUF—TD Reed 19-yard pass from Kelly (Norwood PAT)

NY—TD Toon 19-yard pass from O'Brien (Leahy PAT)

BUF—TD Reed 14-yard pass from Kelly (Norwood PAT)

BUF—FG Norwood 29 yards

NY—FG Leahy 28 yards

BUF—TD Lofton 60-yard pass from Kelly (Norwood PAT)

NY—FG Leahy 25 yards

BUF—TD Mueller 14-yard pass from Kelly (PAT failed)

Jamie Mueller

At practice the day after our comeback win against the Jets, in order to emphasize the importance of all those special-situation drills that I inflicted upon our players, I told them that we would revisit the scramble drill. When we executed it, Kelly seemed to purposely move back and forth an exceedingly large number of times. Finally, he let it fly, and once again he hurled it directly at Jamie Mueller. To the delight of all our players, Mueller dropped it. In the locker room after practice, I walked up to Mueller and asked him if he had done that on purpose. He pled the Fifth Amendment.

The job of fullback is one of the most important and yet unappreciated positions on the team—just ask running backs Thurman Thomas and Kenny Davis. They gain the glamour yards while the fullback is butting heads with linebackers to help pave the way. When the fullback carries—and it isn't often—it's usually against the stacked defenses in short-yardage and goal-line situations, and so his average-per-carry numbers never look impressive. A fullback has to be a good pass receiver because he is often the outlet man when the primary receivers are covered. When he's not out in the pattern, it's up to the fullback to pick up those crazy blitzing linebackers or help out against a great defensive lineman. Jamie Mueller had all those qualities and, besides that, he was one heckuva special teams player. Mueller played a larger role in helping get the Buffalo Bills to the Super Bowl in 1990 than most people realize.

"Mueller played a larger role in helping get the Buffalo Bills to the Super Bowl in 1990 than most people realize." —head coach Marv Levy
(Photo courtesy of Getty Images)

September 7, 2008

Kemp-to-Dubenion, Kelly-to-Reed, Moorman-to-Denney?

Trick Play Fools Seahawks for a Game-Clinching Touchdown on Opening Day

Over the years, the Bills have had some great pass-and-catch combinations. In the '60s, it was Kemp to Dubenion. In the '70s, it was Ferguson to Chandler. In the '80s and '90s, it was Kelly to Reed. In the first decade of the 2000s, it's…Edwards-to-Evans…or is it Moorman-to-Denney?

When punter Brian Moorman hit defensive end Ryan Denney with a 19-yard touchdown pass on a fake field goal in the third quarter of the Bills 2008 opening-day victory over the Seattle Seahawks, he became the first Bills punter ever to throw for a score. Combined with Roscoe Parrish's scintillating punt return for a touchdown in the second quarter and Rian Lindell's two field goals, the Bills special teams accounted for more than two-thirds of the team's points, taking the pressure off an offensive unit

that failed to score at least 20 points in all but four of their games in 2007.

The 2008 season opener was seen as the beginning of a new era in Buffalo, with second-year quarterback Trent Edwards taking over as the starter for former first-stringer J.P. Losman. Edwards came out strong, engineering the Bills' first scoring drive—a four-play, 52-yard march keyed by a 32-yard completion to Lee Evans, which brought the Bills to the Seattle 20. On third-and-11 from the 21, Marshawn Lynch burst through the left side of the line and broke into open space before finding his way into the end zone, giving Buffalo the first lead of the game.

Midway through the second quarter, the Bills forced a Seattle punt, which Roscoe Parrish fielded at his own 37. Parrish zigzagged his way through the Seattle coverage unit and slowed momentarily at the 25 when spun around by Seattle tight end John Carlson, only to break free and outrace three desperate Seahawks into the end zone for a 63-yard touchdown run—his third career touchdown punt return. The Seahawks responded in kind, with quarterback Matt Hasselbeck hitting Nate Burleson with a 20-yard scoring strike to make it 14–7. But two late Rian Lindell field goals gave the Bills a 20–7 lead at the half.

An Olindo Mare field goal closed the chasm to 10 points midway through the third quarter, but the Bills special teams would provide a response on the ensuing

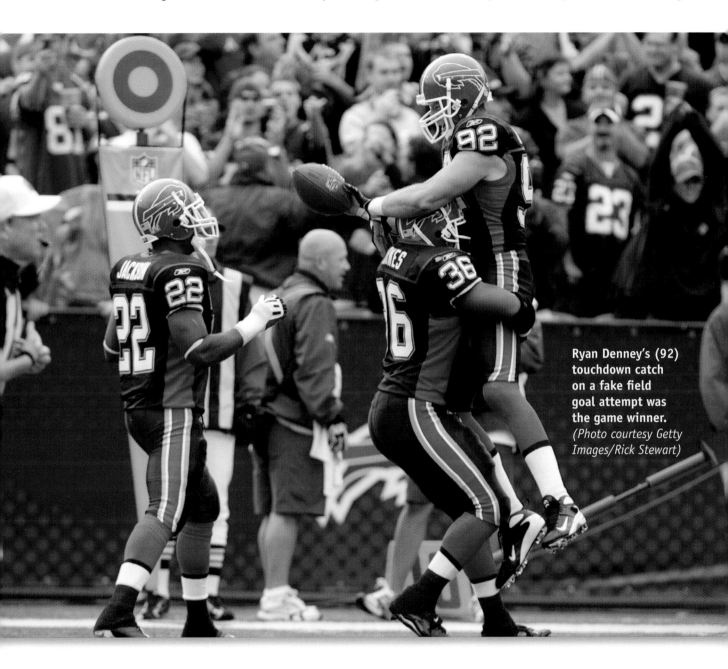

Ryan Denney's (92) touchdown catch on a fake field goal attempt was the game winner. *(Photo courtesy Getty Images/Rick Stewart)*

Game Details

Buffalo Bills 34 • Seattle Seahawks 10

Seahawks	0	7	3	0	**10**
Bills	7	13	14	0	**34**

Date: September 7, 2008

Team Records: Bills 0–0, Seahawks 0–0

Scoring Plays:

BUF—TD Lynch 21-yard run (Lindell PAT)

BUF—TD Parrish 63-yard punt return (Lindell PAT)

SEA—TD Burleson 20-yard pass from Hasselbeck (Mare PAT)

BUF—FG Lindell 35 yards

BUF—FG Lindell 38 yards

SEA—FG Mare 45 yards

BUF—TD Denney 19-yard pass from Moorman (Lindell PAT)

BUF—TD Royal 30-yard pass from Edwards (Lindell PAT)

possession. Starting from the Bills' own 20, Edwards led a sustained drive into Seattle territory, the bulk of the yardage coming on a 41-yard strike to Evans. But the Seahawks defense stiffened, forcing the Bills into a fourth down at the 19. The kicking team was sent onto the field for what appeared to be a run-of-the-mill 36-yard field goal. Denney moved to the left sideline as though he were heading off the field, but then he stopped and lined up as a wide receiver. Somehow, Denney had managed to check in with the official without alerting the Seahawks to the fact he was lurking along the sideline totally uncovered.

"Clearly, it's someone who is not particularly concentrating on that particular play at that particular time," said Seattle's incredulous head coach Mike Holmgren. At the snap, holder Moorman, instead of placing the ball on the ground for Lindell, popped up and threw a floater toward Denney, alone in the flat. The big defensive end pulled in Moorman's throw and raced untouched into the end zone for the touchdown and a 27–10 Buffalo lead.

Roscoe Parrish celebrates with Bills fans after his electrifying punt return for a touchdown in the second quarter. *(Photo courtesy Getty Images/Rick Stewart)*

"I was thinking the whole time they were going to see me over there," Denney said. "Just a great play, and it worked like we wanted it to."

The Bills scored an insurance marker after the Seahawks Josh Wilson fumbled the ensuing kickoff, giving Buffalo the ball at the Seattle 30. Edwards then connected with tight end Robert Royal over the middle for the touchdown, making the final Buffalo 34, Seattle 10.

> **I**t's huge. It's big-time starting off on the right foot. It's good to gain some confidence off this first win of the season and enjoy it while it lasts.
>
> —BILLS QUARTERBACK TRENT EDWARDS

Brian Moorman

One of the most popular Buffalo Bills during the first decade of the 2000s was punter Brian Moorman. Moorman came to the Bills as a free agent in 2001 after having spent two unsuccessful training camps in—ironically enough—the Seattle Seahawks organization and two years with the Berlin Thunder of NFL Europe, where he led the league in punting both seasons. It didn't take long for the Wichita, Kansas, native to establish himself as a fan favorite in Buffalo, where rooters are quick to identify with gritty, lunch-bucket types. Moorman proved himself to be one of those types with his willingness to mix it up by recording three special teams tackles in his first season. In addition to handling the punting duties, Moorman doubled as the team's kickoff specialist, allowing him even greater opportunity to get in on the action.

His 84-yard boot against the Green Bay Packers on December 22, 2002, bested the previous club record of 78 yards set by Paul Maguire in 1969. By 2003, Moorman was beginning to attract notice as one of the top punters in the league after finishing second in the AFC with a 44.6-yard per-punt average, which broke another club mark once held by Maguire, whose 45.5-yard average had stood as the standard for 34 years. In 2005, Moorman broke his own record with an average of 45.7.

After being chosen as a Pro Bowl alternate in 2002 and 2003, Moorman finally got his due with trips to Hawaii in 2006 and 2007. He now holds nearly every significant Bills punting record.

But perhaps more impressive than Moorman's accomplishments on the field are the contributions he has made off it. When it comes to community service, Moorman has been one of the most active players in the history of the franchise, always making himself available to help a charitable cause, especially when it comes to children. Moorman has twice been awarded the Buffalo Bills/Walter Payton Man of the Year Award (2003 and 2009) for community service combined with a high standard of play. In 2005, he received *Pro Football Weekly*'s Arthur S. Arkush Humanitarian of the Year Award for his charitable efforts in the community. Together with his wife Amber, Moorman founded the PUNT Foundation in 2004, which is dedicated to making a difference in the lives of Western New York children facing threatening illnesses. The mission of PUNT (Perseverance, Understanding, N'Couragement, Triumph) is to provide children afflicted with cancer and their families with opportunities to enjoy the life they fight so hard for by supporting pediatric cancer research, treatment, and support groups. Moorman is also active with the Buffalo City Mission, the Food Bank of Western New York, and Roswell Park Cancer Institute, where he and Amber visit regularly to spend time with afflicted children and their families.

September 24, 1989

Kelly-to-Reed TD Beats Oilers in OT

Jim Kelly Connects With His Favorite Target for the Winning Touchdown in Houston

The game was only three minutes old when Scott Norwood put the first points on the board with a 43-yard field goal. The last scoring during the game's regulation 60 minutes came on its last play when Houston kicker Tony Zendejas put one between the uprights from 52 yards away, tying the score and sending the contest into overtime. In between those two field goals, the Bills and Oilers racked up 38 points each, and so we headed into overtime with the score knotted at 41–41.

For the statistics lover, this game was a heavenly delight. The Oilers gained 439 yards from scrimmage, and we countered by ratcheting up 449. Warren Moon put the ball in the air 42 times, and although Jim Kelly had fewer attempts (29), he completed five of them for scores. That means better than one out of every six balls he threw wound up in the end zone. All of this happened on a day when the Oilers had 84 offensive plays to our modest 56, and they controlled the ball 43 minutes to our 28.

There were 23 penalties assessed during the contest, and 13 were against us. And how about Zendejas' kickoffs? He kicked off nine times, and six of them resulted in touchbacks. Seven of our 11 possessions began from either on or inside our own 20. The best drive start we had was from our own 35, and still we scored 47 points.

After Norwood's game-opening field goal, Houston came right back by marching 70 yards to a touchdown. They weren't that fortunate on their next possession, however, because our strong safety, Leonard Smith, intercepted Moon and brought it all the way back to the Houston 23. Three plays later, a pass from Kelly to Thurman Thomas was good for six yards and a touchdown, putting us back in front, 10–7.

Moon was intercepted twice during the contest, and the second one came on their next possession, which Mark Kelso returned 43 yards to the Houston 31. We couldn't turn that one into a touchdown, but Scott nailed a 26-yard field goal to extend the lead to 13–7. Zendejas then responded with a 26-yarder of his own, making it 13–10.

There were only 57 seconds left in the first half as we began our next possession at our own 20. On the first play, Kelly was sacked for a 13-yard loss by William Fuller and Sean Jones. Sensing an opportunity to get the ball back in favorable field position, the Oilers quickly called their first timeout. They did it again after our second down and then used their final timeout of the half after our third down. We punted from our own 8, and they took over at our 39 with 27 seconds remaining. They advanced it to our 29, and on the final play of the half, Zendejas came out to attempt the game-tying field goal. But Darryl Talley blocked it, and Mark Kelso picked it up and raced 77 yards to a touchdown. It wasn't 13–13 after all—it was 20–10 in our favor.

The second half was just as crazy. On our first possession, Kelly teamed up with Don Beebe for a 63-yard beauty. Things were really looking rosy now, but that didn't last. On their next possession, the Oilers answered with a 12-play, 75-yard touchdown drive that narrowed the margin to 27–17. It got even narrower moments later when Bubba McDowell blocked John Kidd's punt deep in our territory. Cris Dishman scooped it up and sprinted into the end zone to pull his team to within three.

Joe Kelly and Andre Reed addressed that problem on the first play of the fourth quarter, hooking up for a sensational 78-yard touchdown bomb. The score was now 34–24. But the Oilers quelled our mirth with an

For the day, receiver Andre Reed had five receptions for 135 yards and two touchdowns. *(Photo courtesy Getty Images/Craig R. Melvin)*

eight-play, 78-yard touchdown drive of their own, the final 26 yards coming on a pass from Moon to wide receiver Ernest Givens (one of nine receivers to whom Moon distributed passes this day). It got worse on our next series when defensive back Steve Brown intercepted Kelly's pass at the Buffalo 48-yard line and took it all the way down to the 7. Three plays later, Lorenzo White scored on a one-yard plunge, and with just 4:40 remaining, Houston had taken a 38–34 lead.

Things looked grim as we began our last possession of regulation at our own 17. But Kelly willed us as far as the Houston 26 before being sacked once again by that danged Fuller, putting us in a third-and-16 situation. But so what? On the next play, it was Kelly to Thomas for 26 yards and another Buffalo touchdown. We had retaken the lead, 41–38, and there was only 1:52 left. For Moon and the Oilers, however, that was an eternity.

It was for us, too, as the Oilers squeezed 10 plays into that limited time frame. They could only advance it as far as our 34, but Zendejas nailed a 52-yarder as time expired. We were going into overtime. How much can your nerves take?

We lost the doggone coin toss. One had to wonder whether we'd ever get the ball, because Moon engineered an 11-play drive that took the Oilers from their own 19 all the way to our 20, where we forced a fourth-and-11. Zendejas, the man who had made a game-tying 52-yard field goal just six minutes earlier came onto the field now to attempt the game-winner from 37 yards out. We let out a collective sigh as the kick sailed wide.

> **Y**ou've got the two best quarterbacks playing at the top of their game, [so] you're going to have a lot of points scored. Those guys put on a show that should be bottled.
>
> —BILLS DEFENSIVE TACKLE FRED SMERLAS

Kelly then took control. Starting at our own 20, Kelly completed three straight passes to advance the ball into Houston territory. A 13-yard scramble then took us to their 28. The Oilers came with an all-out blitz, leaving Andre Reed facing one-on-one coverage. Kelly read it perfectly, hitting Reed in the left flat at the 22. Reed made a quick juke that left the Houston defensive backs flat-footed, and he sprinted into the end zone for the game-winning score.

It was Kelly's fifth touchdown pass of the game, and Andre's fifth reception—two of them for touchdowns—for 135 yards.

It was a great plane ride home.

Game Details

Buffalo Bills 47 • Houston Oilers 41 (OT)

Bills	10	10	7	14	6	**47**
Oilers	7	3	14	17	0	**41**

Date: September 24, 1989

Team Records: Bills 1–1, Oilers 1–1

Scoring Plays:

BUF—FG Norwood 43 yards

HOU—TD Moon 1-yard run (Zendejas PAT)

BUF—TD Thomas 6-yard pass from Kelly (Norwood PAT)

BUF—FG Norwood 26 yards

HOU—FG Zendejas 26 yards

BUF—TD Kelso 76-yard blocked field goal return (Norwood PAT)

BUF—TD Beebe 63-yard pass from Kelly (Norwood PAT)

HOU—TD Highsmith 4-yard run (Zendejas PAT)

BUF—TD Reed 78-yard pass from Kelly (Norwood PAT)

HOU—TD Givins 26-yard pass from Moon (Zendejas PAT)

HOU—TD White 1-yard run (Zendejas PAT)

BUF—TD Thomas 26-yard pass from Kelly (Norwood PAT)

HOU—FG Zendejas 52 yards

BUF—TD Reed 28-yard pass from Kelly in overtime (No PAT attempt)

Andre Reed

He never bragged—he just performed. Quietly, Andre Reed racked up eye-popping statistics, but he was never the one to tell you about it. He is one of the greatest wide receivers ever to play the game, and the recognition he deserves for his play and his modesty must come from others. If ever a player merited selection for induction into the Pro Football Hall of Fame, Reed is that player. The winning touchdown he caught in that overtime victory against Houston is just one of so many game-winners he contributed during his remarkable career.

Reed joined the Bills in 1985 as a relatively unknown fourth-round draft choice out of Kutztown State University in Pennsylvania. Even to the Bills he seemed to have been an afterthought. In that year's draft, the Bills had already picked six players prior to calling out his name, and one of those preceding six was a wide receiver. Fifteen glorious years later, including seven Pro Bowl appearances, Reed's days in Buffalo finally came to an end. When that day arrived, no one in the history of the NFL, except for Jerry Rice and Tim Brown, had more career receptions than Reed. He still ranks fourth all-time with 951 receptions—87 of them for touchdowns.

Both of those figures, of course, are Buffalo Bills team records, along with his all-time receiving-yards-gained total of 13,198, which ranks sixth on the NFL all-time list. Those yards came not just because he made the catch but because of the talent and courage Reed possessed when called upon to come bursting across the middle to make those difficult catches and then to do something about it afterward. His nickname of "Yac" wasn't bestowed upon him because he talked a lot. It was a product of his unique ability and desire to rack up those "Yards After Catch" stats.

Reed holds other Bills records: most games with 100 yards or more receiving (36); most catches in a single game (15); tied with offensive lineman Jim Ritcher for most regular-season games played (221); tied with Bruce Smith for the longest-tenured player in the team's existence (15 years). Those are just some of his records.

Does Andre Reed belong in the Pro Football Hall of Fame? You betcha!

Wide receiver Andre Reed caught a 28-yard touchdown pass for the winning score.
(Photo courtesy Getty Images/ Al Messerschmidt)

October 26, 1992

Late Pass to Thomas Saves the Day (Night)

Thomas Caps Huge Monday Night Performance with Game-Winning Touchdown

It had been a hard-fought, back-and-forth battle. And at the close of the third period, Steve Christie's 33-yard field goal extended the Bills lead over the Jets to a precarious 17–13. We had succeeded in thwarting three New York possessions in the fourth quarter but had little success in moving the ball ourselves, and likewise failed to score on our three drives. With just 3:38 remaining to be played, we were forced to punt it away, and the Jets took over at their own 23-yard line.

They moved into our territory and on a first-and-10 at our 45, Jets quarterback Ken O'Brien lofted a bomb deep along the right sideline. It was intended for wide receiver Rob Moore, who was being closely covered by cornerback James Williams. The pass fell incomplete in the end zone, but before the play ended it turned out that the football wasn't the only article that fluttered in the air. An official's yellow flag— signifying pass interference against our defender and greeted with a roar of approval by the assembled Jets fans—was also part of the scene. It was New York's ball, first-and-goal on our 1-yard line. On the next play, Jets fullback Brad Baxter took it over for the score that put his team in front 20–17 with just 1:50 left on the play clock.

The season that had begun so magnificently seemed to be heading south in a hurry. We had come into the season as two-time defending AFC champions, and after

Running back Thurman Thomas averaged more than six yards per carry as the Bills defeated the Jets.
(Photo courtesy Getty Images/Jim Turner/NFL)

storming to victories in our first four games—while averaging better than 38 points a game—we had lost the next two against Miami and the Los Angeles Raiders. We were now on the brink of extending that losing streak to three…but not in the eyes of one of the greatest team leaders who ever played the game. I recall Jim Kelly walking alone in front of the bench immediately after the Jets scored their go-ahead touchdown, saying to his teammates, "If we don't get our butts in gear, we aren't going to win this damn game."

They responded, and so did he. During our final desperate possession on that autumn evening, things did not start out well. On first-and-10 at our own 25, Jets defensive end Marvin Washington sacked Kelly for an eight-yard loss. It got a little better after that. On second-and-18, Kelly hit Don Beebe coming across the middle, and the speediest man on our team turned it into a 34-yard gain before running out of bounds. After throwing incompletions on first and second down, it was once again Kelly to Beebe, this time for a 19-yard gain that took the ball down to the Jets 30.

A field goal now could tie the score. The Buffalo Bills and Jim Kelly, however, weren't thinking field goal. With less than a minute remaining to be played, Kelly lined up in a shotgun formation, but instead of passing, he slipped the ball to Thurman Thomas, who proceeded to race 18 yards for another first down at the Jets 12. That was Thomas' 21st carry of the game, and it brought his rushing total up to 142 yards—an average of 6.8 yards per carry.

Despite all the heroics for which Thurman had been responsible, we still trailed, and the game clock was ticking inexorably toward its final destination. The dynamic duo of Kelly and Thomas changed all that on the next play. Kelly hit Thurman over the middle, and No. 34 bulled his way the final two yards into the end zone for the winning touchdown. Buffalo Bills 24, New York Jets 20.

This ability to come back from dire circumstances became the signature quality of the 1992 Buffalo Bills. It rescued us from what would have been our third consecutive loss, and instead it became the first in a streak of five straight wins. It was also the season in which our players, during the Wild Card Playoff Game against the Houston Oilers two-and-a-half months later, rallied from a 35–3 deficit and startled the football world by winning that game in overtime—the greatest comeback in NFL history.

Game Details

Buffalo Bills 24 • New York Jets 20

Bills	0	14	3	7	**24**
Jets	3	3	7	7	**20**

Date: October 26, 1992

Team Records: Bills 4–2, Jets 1–5

Scoring Plays:

NY—FG Blanchard 42 yards
BUF—TD K. Davis 2-yard run (Christie PAT)
NY—FG Blanchard 40 yards
BUF—TD Lofton 16-yard pass from Kelly (Christie PAT)
NY—TD Chaffey 1-yard run (Blanchard PAT)
BUF—FG Christie 33 yards
NY—TD Baxter 1-yard run (Blanchard PAT)
BUF—TD Thomas 12-yard pass from Kelly (Christie PAT)

> **W**hen it comes down to it, when you have to make the big play, you make it. I just said, 'Guys, I know we can do it. Let's just put it all together.'
>
> —BILLS QUARTERBACK JIM KELLY

Thurman Thomas

Thurman Thomas had, in my mind, the single most important quality of a great running back, and that's balance. You hit him, and you would just knock him sideways. He could easily regain his balance when he was hit. Because of his balance, he had the ability to cut. He had great discretion—when to turn it on, when to go outside, when to cut back, when to lunge forward. Beyond that, he was a magnificent receiver. Despite not having been a pass receiving back in college, by the time his playing days were concluded, Thomas had gone on to become the second all-time leading receiver in Bills history. And when called upon to block, he could do the dirty work, too. He was truly an amazing athlete.

Thurman Thomas rushed his way into the Pro Football Hall of Fame. *(Photo courtesy Getty Images/Jim Turner/NFL)*

Don Beebe

Aside from Jim Kelly and Thurman Thomas, there was one other offensive player who played a huge role in the success we enjoyed that Monday night in the Meadowlands, and he wasn't even in the starting lineup. Don Beebe, our third receiver behind Andre Reed and James Lofton, caught six passes in the game for a total of 106 yards. His catches and his ability to run after making the catch were vital components in helping us emerge victorious. On our final and winning drive, Beebe contributed receptions of 34 and 19 yards. The first one came on a second-and-18 situation, while the second bailed us out of a third-and-10, thereby keeping alive the drive—and our hopes of winning.

Defensive Standouts

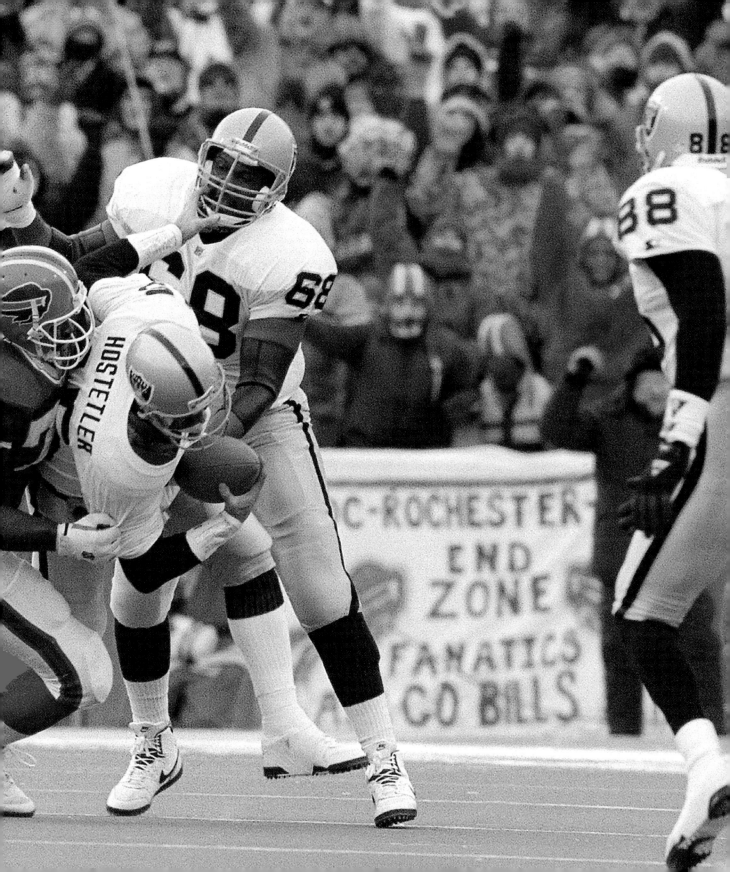

December 26, 1964

The Hit Heard 'Round the World

Stratton KOs Lincoln to Steal Momentum in AFL Title Game

The image is seared into the collective memory of longtime fans of the Buffalo Bills. Robert Smith's iconic shot of Mike Stratton a split-second away from destroying Keith Lincoln's ribs in the 1964 AFL Title Game is arguably the most famous action photograph in the league's history, and it captured the defining moment of the Bills' AFL era.

The 1964 title game was the culmination of the most successful season in the Bills' five-year existence. The 12–2 record posted by the Bills was the best in the league. And the defense, the centerpiece of the team, was one of the most dominant ever fielded, yielding a league-low 242 points and going the last eight regular-season games without giving up a rushing touchdown. The team with the next-best record, the San Diego Chargers at 8–5–1, was to be their opponent in the title game. However, despite their dominance over the league that year, the advantage of playing at their home field of War Memorial Stadium, and the Chargers not having their biggest weapon—wide receiver Lance Alworth—the Bills still entered the game as the underdogs.

The Chargers came ready to play, as evidenced by defensive tackle Earl Faison's declaration prior to the kickoff. "San Diego was on one side of the field, and we were on the other," said Bills cornerback Butch Byrd. "We were huddled up, and Lou Saban was giving us a 'rah rah' speech. From out of nowhere, Faison leaned into our huddle and said, 'You guys better play—I'm gonna kill somebody today!' And Faison was huge. I just looked at him. Everyone looked at him. He was just wide-eyed."

The Chargers received the opening kick and made it clear on their first possession that they planned to pound it out on the ground. Keith Lincoln went 38 yards on a first-down draw, then carried again for five more. Two plays later, quarterback Tobin Rote hit tight end Dave Kocourek for a 26-yard touchdown and the game's first lead. Things were not looking promising for the Bills, who were forced to punt on their next possession. But everything was about to change—dramatically so—courtesy of Buffalo's All-Pro linebacker Mike Stratton.

The Chargers had possession when, on second-and-10 from their own 34, Rote called for a flair pass to Lincoln in the left flat. As Stratton recalled, "They seemed to have a pattern that they ran where they would flair the back out of the backfield behind the line of scrimmage. At the same time, they would run the wide receiver on a curl, and then they would key on the linebacker. If the linebacker came up to cover the back, they would automatically throw to the curl. If the linebacker went back to cover the curl, they would throw to the back."

After the Chargers ran the play a couple of times, Stratton responded. "When the pattern came again, I just turned my head and started running for the outside receiver. After I ran about four or five steps, I turned around and looked back and started back toward the flair back. I had run far enough to discourage them—I'd better go for the back."

Robert Stratton's punishing hit on Keith Lincoln knocked the Chargers' running back out of the 1964 AFL title game and turned the contest in the Bills' favor. (Photo courtesy Robert L. Smith, Orchard Park, NY)

"Rote was looking for someone else and then dumped it off to Lincoln," Byrd recalled. "It looked like Lincoln had clear sailing. The ball kind of floated out there, and Mike, with his great speed, just closed on Lincoln. I was watching the ball, and I was watching Lincoln, and I could see they were going to get there at the same time."

"I saw the ball in the air," Stratton said, "and I was running like the devil to get to the back before he caught the ball and was able to juke me and pick up the first down. I knew it was going to be close. I got to Lincoln about the same time the ball did, and that was that. I knew it was a substantial collision."

"What an explosion!" Byrd said. "He hit Lincoln, and I think Lincoln was shot."

Lincoln was removed from the field, his ribs—along with the Chargers thunder—fractured.

According to All-Pro guard Billy Shaw, the Stratton hit completely changed the complexion of the game. "When Mike made this play, that turned things around. Up until that point, they had the momentum. They had already scored. Because Keith was gone, we had a chance."

"Stratton's hit turned the game around," said fullback Wray Carlton. "Lincoln was having a great year and was

Chargers halfback Keith Lincoln was removed from the game with fractured ribs. *(Photo courtesy Getty Images/Fred Roe/NFL)*

really their offense. After he went out, they definitely lost their best weapon. What it did was deflate them."

No doubt about it. On their next possession, the Bills drove 64 yards in six plays to their first points of the game, a 12-yard Pete Gogolak field goal, and from there it was all Buffalo. The Bills scored 20 unanswered points en route to a 20–7 thrashing of the favored Chargers and the first of two AFL titles. It might have been completely different had Stratton not sniffed out San Diego's tendency and knocked Lincoln out of the game.

"When it was over," Stratton observed, "that's when it would dawn on everybody that we actually accomplished what we had set out to do."

> The Stratton hit actually turned the key. From that point on, we felt we did have a chance to win it. Mike's hit was a display of defensive strength. It lit the flame.
>
> —HEAD COACH LOU SABAN

Game Details

Buffalo Bills 20 • San Diego Chargers 7

Chargers	7	0	0	0	7
Bills	3	10	0	7	20

Date: December 26, 1964

Team Records: Bills 12–2, Chargers 8–5–1

Scoring Plays:

SD—TD Kocourek 26-yard pass from Rote (Lincoln PAT)

BUF—FG Gogolak 12 yards

BUF—TD Carlton 4-yard run (Gogolak PAT)

BUF—FG Gogolak 17 yards

BUF—TD Kemp 1-yard run (Gogolak PAT)

Mike Stratton

Mike Stratton (13th-round pick, 1962, University of Tennessee), the man who made The Hit Heard 'Round the World when he flattened the Chargers star running back Keith Lincoln in the 1964 title game, was a tight end and defensive end in college, but he was switched to linebacker during his first training camp. "When the coach called everybody's name when we were going out, he didn't call my name," Stratton later recalled of his first day at practice. "I said, 'Where do you want me to go?' He said, 'What is your name again?' I figured I was in a little bit of trouble at that time. He said, 'Why don't you go with the defensive ends?' So I went out with the defensive ends. Then apparently they got several linebackers hurt, and they switched me to linebacker, and I couldn't have been happier."

Nor could the Bills. Stratton developed into one of the premier linebackers in the league, appearing in six consecutive AFL All-Star games between 1964–69. The Bills' linebacker corps of Stratton, John Tracey, and Harry Jacobs started 62 consecutive games together from 1962–67. During his 11 years with the team, Stratton chalked up 18 interceptions (including six in his rookie season alone) and scored two safeties. He was the last remaining link to the franchise's glory years when he was traded to, ironically enough, the San Diego Chargers prior to the 1973 season. Stratton was named to the All-Time AFL Team as an outside linebacker (second squad) by the Pro Football Hall of Fame Selection Committee in 1969. Truly one of the Bills' all-time greats, Stratton was enshrined on the team's Wall of Fame in 1994 and in the Greater Buffalo Sports Hall of Fame in 2005.

January 31, 1993

Beebe Never Gives Up

Don Beebe Chases Down Leon Lett to Thwart Touchdown in Super Bowl XXVII

It was one of the most painful days in Buffalo Bills history. We were being humiliated. True, much of that humiliation was our own doing, but it still hurt. With less than five minutes remaining to be played in Super Bowl XXVII, we were losing to the Dallas Cowboys by a score of 52–17. If you looked merely at some of the statistics, it would be hard to imagine that such a disparity in the score could be happening. When it was all over, we had registered more first downs than the Cowboys (22–20). We had converted 45 percent of our third downs (5-of-11), same as the Cowboys. We had gained 362 yards on offense. Wide receiver Andre Reed had turned in yet another outstanding performance with eight receptions for 152 yards, topping all receivers in the game.

We limited the Cowboys to a single yard on their first possession. When they punted, Steve Tasker showed them why he was the best kicking-teams player to ever play the game. Tasker blocked Mike Saxon's punt, and we recovered the ball at the Dallas 16. Four plays later—all of them runs by Thurman Thomas—Thurman took it in from the 2. Less than five minutes into the game, we had a 7–0 lead. It didn't last long. On our next possession, Jim Kelly was intercepted by safety James Washington. Six plays later, Troy Aikman completed a 23-yard touchdown toss to tight end Jay Novacek. The score was tied.

A penalty on the ensuing kickoff forced us to start our next drive from our own 10-yard line. We weren't going to get conservative, so we came out passing. But defensive end Charles Haley sacked Kelly at the 2, stripping him of the ball. Jimmie Jones picked it up and tiptoed into our end zone. Dallas 14, Buffalo 7. The next time we got the ball, we marched all the way to their 1 but failed to make it on fourth-and-goal. Our next possession began on our own 15, and Kelly got us as far as our 33 before spraining his knee on a throw to Reed. Kelly was out for the rest of the game. Frank Reich took over, and our drive continued. Once again, we got as far as the Dallas 1 and faced a fourth-down situation. I decided to go for the points, and Steve Christie's field goal closed the gap to 14–10. There was 3:24 left in the half and, as the score indicated, it was a tight battle. That was all about to change.

After we kicked off, the Cowboys put together a 72-yard scoring drive that Aikman finished with a 19-yard pass to Michael Irvin to make it 21–10. We fumbled away our next possession, and it was Aikman to Irvin again, this time from 18 yards out to give Dallas a 28–10 lead that remained until intermission.

In that first half, we had turned the ball over five times (three interceptions and two lost fumbles). Dallas hadn't turned it over once. Oh well, at least we had blocked a punt.

To begin the second half, the Cowboys drove 77 yards to our 2, but we stiffened and they settled for a 20-yard field goal. Late in the third quarter, Reich completed a 40-yard scoring strike to Don Beebe, and we entered the fourth period trailing 31–17. We still had a fighting chance. Early in the period, Bruce Smith slammed into Emmitt Smith at the Cowboys 30 and the ball came flying out. It was one of those days, however, in which we couldn't even recover the other team's fumbles. Aikman fell on it, and Dallas retained possession. A couple of

Leon Lett (78) thinks he has an easy touchdown, but Don Beebe (82) is about to spoil his fun.
(Photo courtesy Getty Images/Dave Cross/NFL)

minutes later, an Aikman-to-Alvin Harper strike made it 38–17.

The rout was on. We had to take big chances now. And this time, they didn't pay off. During the next three minutes of play we suffered one interception, a fumble lost on a quarterback sack, and another lost by a receiver after making the catch. The Cowboys converted two of them into touchdowns, 45–17. Wait—make that 52–17.

Time was running out. The win was wrapped up for the Cowboys, but there was no way the Buffalo Bills wouldn't keep trying. On a drive that reached the Dallas 31, Reich dropped back to pass. Cowboys defensive end Jim Jeffcoat got to him and knocked the ball loose. His teammate, Leon Lett, scooped it up and set sail for our goal line 64 yards away. There was no one between Lett and one more Dallas touchdown. The instant the ball came out of Reich's hands,

> **I** wasn't going to quit. The way I've been taught in high school and college and by Marv Levy is if you can make a play, then make it. I was determined to catch the guy and try to knock the ball out. Then when he started celebrating around the 10-yard line, I knew I was going to catch him.
>
> —BILLS WIDE RECEIVER DON BEEBE

Beebe, 25 yards downfield on a pass pattern, began sprinting back in the direction of the line of scrimmage. There was no one on the field as fast as Beebe, but it still seemed futile for him to be giving pursuit when he started so far from his quarry. No one thought he had a chance of catching Lett—no one, that is, except Beebe.

As Lett raced unimpeded across our 5-yard line, he raised the ball in the air in triumphant anticipation of crossing into the promised land. At the 1, the streaking Beebe leapt into the air from behind and knocked the ball out of Lett's hands into the end zone. We recovered it there for a touchback. It was our ball at the 20.

Moments later the game ended. It really didn't make much difference whether we lost that game by a score of 59–17 or by a score of 52–17, did it? In this instance, the answer is yes, it did make a difference. It sent a message to the entire football world that the Buffalo Bills would never quit. It reaffirmed in the minds of all of our players and coaches that this was the most resilient group of athletes who ever came up the tunnel and onto the playing field. And it set the tone for the season that lay ahead, when our Bills would battle their way back to the Super Bowl for the fourth consecutive year.

In this final game of a season in which we had consistently won the turnover battle on our way to our third straight Super Bowl appearance, we were about to embark on an unparalleled reversal of that modus operandi. Before it was all over, we turned the ball over an unprecedented nine—that's right, nine—times. Given that figure, it's remarkable that we were able to hold the Cowboys to just 52 points.

Game Details

Dallas Cowboys 52 • Buffalo Bills 17

Bills	7	3	7	0	**17**
Cowboys	14	14	3	21	**52**

Date: January 31, 1993

Team records: Bills 11–5, Cowboys 13–3

Scoring Plays:

BUF—TD Thomas 2-yard run (Christie PAT)

DAL—TD Novacek 23-yard pass from Aikman (Elliott PAT)

DAL—TD Jones 2-yard fumble return (Elliott PAT)

BUF—FG Christie 21 yards

DAL—TD Irvin 19-yard pass from Aikman (Elliott PAT)

DAL—TD Irvin 18-yard pass from Aikman (Elliott PAT)

DAL—FG Elliott 20 yards

BUF—TD Beebe 40-yard pass from Reich (Christie PAT)

DAL—TD Harper 45-yard pass from Aikman (Elliott PAT)

DAL—TD E. Smith 10-yard run (Elliott PAT)

DAL—TD Norton 9-yard fumble return (Elliott PAT)

Bills receiver Don Beebe knocked the ball away from Cowboys defensive tackle Leon Lett to prevent a touchdown in Super Bowl **XXVII.** *(Photo courtesy Getty Images/NFL)*

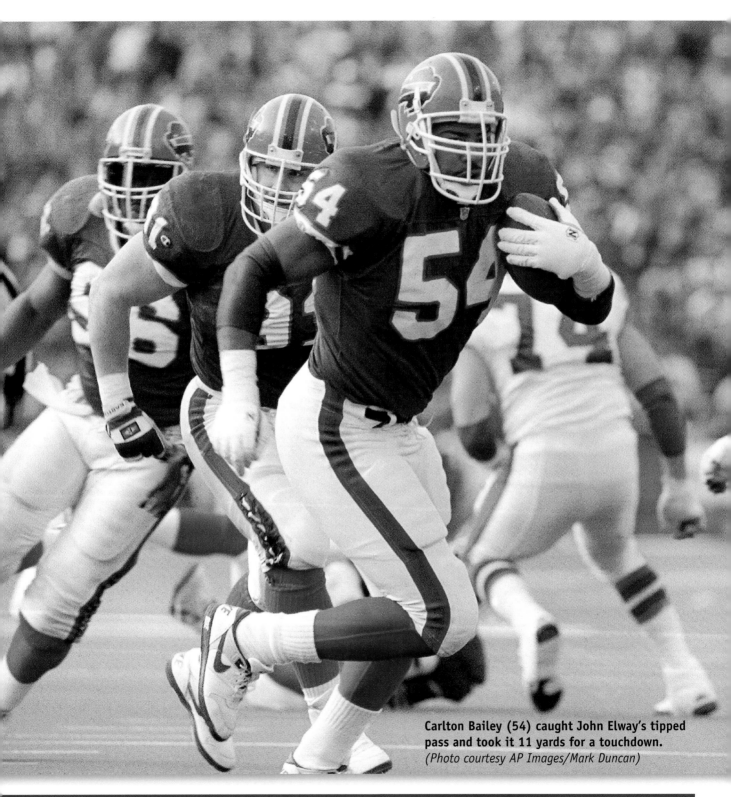

Carlton Bailey (54) caught John Elway's tipped pass and took it 11 yards for a touchdown.
(Photo courtesy AP Images/Mark Duncan)

January 12, 1992

Bailey the Unlikely Hero

Carlton Bailey Returns Elway's Pass for Touchdown to Give Bills Second Straight AFC Title

It had only been a year since we romped to the AFC championship by routing the Los Angeles Raiders at Rich Stadium by a score of 51–3. Once again in our home stadium, with our high-powered offense primed and eager, we were playing for that title. This time it was against the Denver Broncos, and all signs pointed to a shootout between Hall of Fame-to-be quarterbacks John Elway and Jim Kelly. Well, that's what the experts predicted anyway. But boy, were they wrong! Ten minutes into the third quarter, the score was still 0–0. Two super defenses, winds of 25 mph—including even more aggressive gusts—and some weird circumstances all conspired to make the fans wonder whether they were watching an NFL game or a soccer match.

During the first half, our vaunted offense managed a total of 58 yards. On six of our eight possessions, we were off the field in three plays or less. We converted just one of seven third downs and had turned the ball over on an interception at our own 29-yard line. Adding to all that, Denver

had a time-of-possession advantage of 21 minutes to our nine. Now you know why we hadn't scored any points, but what in the world kept the Broncos from doing so?

Early in the first quarter Denver had marched to our 34, but our defense threw them for three consecutive losses—a one-yard stuffing of a running play by Darryl Talley, a four-yard loss when Leon Seals penetrated their backfield to stop a draw play, and a 12-yard loss when nose tackle Jeff Wright sacked Elway on third-and-15. The Broncos punted. Two plays later, they got it back when Kelly's pass was tipped at the line of scrimmage and linebacker Greg Kragen intercepted at our 29. Our challenged defense stopped them again, and when David Treadwell's 47-yard field goal attempt went wide left, the scoreboard remained unchanged.

The next time the Broncos took possession, they drove all the way from their own 24 deep into our territory. On a second-and-6 from our 11, Bruce Smith spilled Elway for a five-yard loss. On the next play, it was "Bruuuuuuuuce!" again as he sacked Elway for an eight-yard loss. Treadwell then trotted onto the field for his second attempt. On this one, he compensated for the previous wide-left miss by aiming a bit more to the right. The swirling wind continued to play tricks, and the 42-yard try banged into the right upright and bounced back out. Nothing to nothing.

We were forced to punt away our next possession, and the Broncos took over at midfield. They got as far as our 20 this time. Treadwell was called upon once again, but his 37-yard effort yielded the same result. It hit the right upright again and bounced our way. It remained 0–0 as the first half ended.

We finally got some offense going in the third quarter, moving the ball from our own 20 all the way to the Denver 26 in 11 plays. But the drive came to an abrupt halt when cornerback Tyrone Braxton intercepted Kelly at the 19. I have always maintained, however, that what you do after a giveaway or a takeaway is what is really reflective of the character of the players on your team. Jeff Wright and Carlton Bailey must have been listening intently whenever I chanted that mantra. On second-and-10, Elway dropped back to pass. It was going to be a screen pass, and nose tackle Wright analyzed it immediately. Instead of continuing his rush, Wright fell back, shot his hand up, and deflected the pass just as Elway released the ball. Linebacker Bailey, who was streaking to carry out his man-to-man coverage assignment, plucked it out of the air and cruised 11 exciting yards for the touchdown. We were in front, 7–0, but the game was a long way from over.

On Denver's last series of the quarter, Elway was shaken up and had to leave the game. They would have to play the final stanza with backup Gary Kubiak at the controls, and what a performance he turned in. During the final 12:49 of the game, he completed 11-of-12 pass attempts for 136 yards and rushed three times for 22 more. And yet we won the game. How could that be? On Kubiak's first drive, the Broncos moved from their own 21 deep into our territory. On a fourth-and-11 at our 33—a situation made possible by Darryl Talley's sack for a loss of 10 on the previous play—Kubiak connected with wide receiver Mike Young, but a stop-you-now tackle by our dime back, Clifford Hicks, kept them one yard shy of the first down. Our ball.

We marched as far as the Denver 26, and from there Scott Norwood—wind be damned—kicked a 44-yard field goal. We were in front now by a score of 10–0. There was only 4:09 remaining, and Elway was out of the game. We've got it wrapped up now, haven't we? The longest four minutes of the season were about to begin.

Eight plays and two-and-a-half minutes later, Kubiak, on a three-yard keeper, capped an 85-yard drive to make it 10–7. There was 1:38 left to play when Treadwell made up for his earlier errant field goal attempts by kicking a perfect onside kickoff. It was recovered at midfield by Denver free safety Steve Atwater. It seemed disaster was closing in on us. On first down, Kubiak completed yet another pass, this one to Steve Sewell at our 44. But it was there that cornerback Kirby Jackson saved our season. He applied a jarring tackle that dislodged the ball from Sewell's grip and recovered the loose pigskin.

We were on our way back to the Super Bowl.

> **I** was just trying to score. The linebackers would have been all over me if I hadn't scored.
>
> —BILLS LINEBACKER CARLTON BAILEY

Game Details

Buffalo Bills 10 • Denver Broncos 7

Broncos	0	0	0	7	**7**
Bills	0	0	7	3	**10**

Date: January 12, 1992

Team Records: Bills 13–3, Broncos 12–4

Scoring Plays:

BUF—TD Bailey 11-yard interception return (Norwood PAT)

BUF—FG Norwood 44 yards

DEN—TD Kubiak 3-yard run (Treadwell PAT)

Carlton Bailey

Carlton Bailey was the Bills ninth-round pick in 1988. He was actually a nose tackle while at the University of North Carolina and even won the Lawrence Taylor Award as UNC's top defensive player in his senior year.

We turned the 6'3", 242-pounder into an inside linebacker in his first training camp with the Bills, but he spent his first three seasons in the shadows of our other somewhat better known linebackers. (You may have heard of them—guys with names like Cornelius Bennett, Ray Bentley, Shane Conlan, and Darryl Talley.) Bailey proved most valuable to us on special teams, where he played a key role in the success of one of the best squads ever assembled.

Bailey eventually found his way into the starting lineup, taking over at right inside linebacker in 1991 and becoming a formidable run-stuffer. But the fiscal realities of professional sports caused us to lose this fine young man after the 1992 season when he signed a huge free-agent contract to play for the New York Giants. At the time, he became the Giants' highest-paid linebacker, exceeding even the salaries of All-Pro Carl Banks and future Hall of Famer Lawrence Taylor.

When former Bills general manager Bill Polian assumed the same position with the expansion Carolina Panthers in 1994, his first order of business was to accumulate players to fill out the team's roster for its inaugural season in 1995. Like me, Polian has always believed that the foundation of any successful sports team lies in the character of its players. With that in mind, and with a blatant disregard for sentimentality, Polian raided the roster he had helped build in Buffalo and signed quarterback Frank Reich, wide receiver Don Beebe, and tight end Pete Metzelaars. Polian also made a point of signing Carlton Bailey, and this proved to be the most important acquisition of all of the former Bills— when the Panthers went to the playoffs in just their second year in existence, he was the only ex-Bill left on the team.

Bailey enjoyed three solid years with the Panthers before retiring after the 1997 season.

Linebacker Carlton Bailey was around the ball all day as the Bills won their second straight AFC title.
(Photo courtesy Getty Images/ Rick Stewart/Allsport)

December 27, 1981

Simpson's Interception Secures Thrilling Playoff Win

Safety's Last-Minute Theft Ices Jets and Allows Bills to Advance to Next Round

It had been a long time coming—16 years, in fact. The Bills had not been victorious in the postseason since defeating the San Diego Chargers in the AFL Title Game in 1965. It's no surprise then that this victory in the 1981 AFC Wild Card Playoff Game is remembered as one of the biggest in franchise history. The way it came about made it one for the ages.

The Bills exploded out of the box, building up a 24–0 lead before the Jets knew what hit them. It started right from the opening kickoff when linebacker Ervin Parker forced returner Bruce Harper to fumble. Charles Romes alertly gathered it in at the Jets 26 and brought it back for the score and a 7–0 lead just 16 seconds into the action. The lead grew to 14–0 midway through the first, when Joe Ferguson collaborated with Frank Lewis on a 50-yard catch-and-run to pay dirt. Rufus Bess killed the Jets next possession by intercepting quarterback Richard Todd and making a 49-yard return. Nick Mike-Mayer then kicked a 29-yard field goal, and the Bills had a shocking 17–0 first-quarter advantage.

The lead grew to 24–0 late in the second after an interception by linebacker Phil Villipiano gave the Bills possession at their own 41. Five plays later, Ferguson hit Lewis from 26 yards out, but it was a spectacular 28-yard reception by Joe Cribbs that keyed the drive. The Jets awoke from their slumber on their next possession, as Todd led a 53-yard, four-play drive that culminated in a 30-yard strike to tight end Mickey Shuler. The Bills ensuing drive was cut short when Greg Buttle intercepted Ferguson at the Buffalo 43 and brought it back to the 14. Buffalo's defense stiffened, forcing the Jets to settle for a 26-yard Leahy field goal that cut the deficit to 14 points. Buttle repeated the deed by picking off another Ferguson pass later in the period, giving the Jets a first down at the Buffalo 8. On third-and-goal from the 1, Todd was thrown for a loss, and once again the Jets came away with only a Leahy field goal to show for their efforts.

Rather than playing conservatively as they entered the fourth quarter with a 24–13 lead, the Bills came out throwing, leading to Ferguson's third interception on the day, this time by defensive back Donald Dykes. Free safety

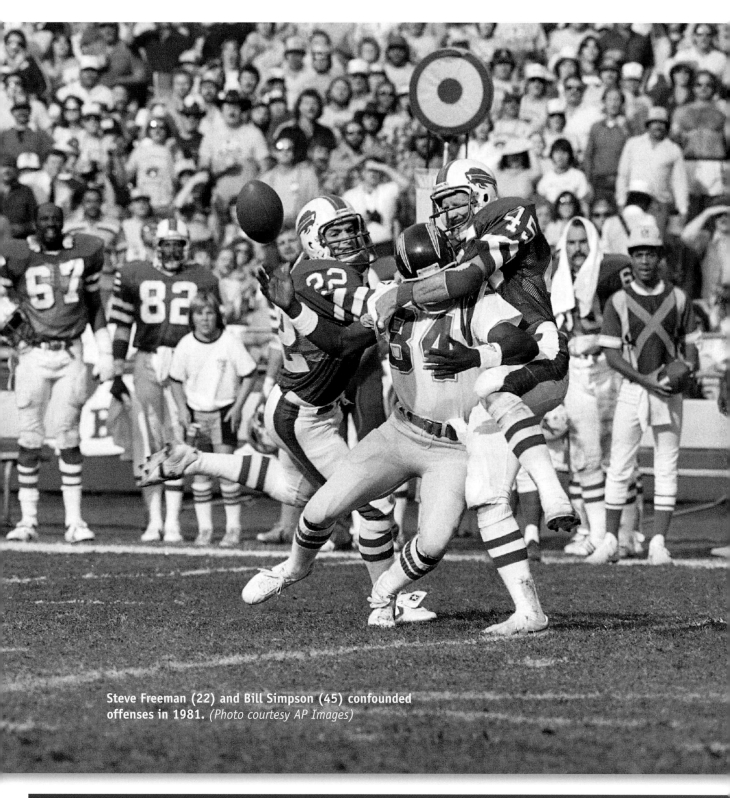

Steve Freeman (22) and Bill Simpson (45) confounded offenses in 1981. *(Photo courtesy AP Images)*

Bill Simpson turned the tables on the Jets by picking off Todd, but then Ferguson threw his fourth interception of the half. Buffalo's stingy defense forced a Jets punt, and the Bills took over at the New York 45. On first down, Cribbs took Ferguson's pitchout, cut around the right end, and broke free for the touchdown that gave the Bills a seemingly insurmountable 31–13 lead with 10:16 to go.

The Jets, however, weren't giving up that easily. Taking possession at their own 20, the Jets took 3:02 to march to Todd's second touchdown pass of the game, this one for 30 yards to wide receiver Bobby Jones, closing the chasm to 11 points. The Jets defense—the so-called New York Sack Exchange—forced the Bills into a three-and-out, and Todd went back to work from his own 42 with 5:43 remaining in regulation. Fred Smerlas sacked Todd on first down, then Mario Clark killed the drive with an interception—or so it seemed. Clark had been flagged for pass interference, and the Jets were given the ball back with a new set of downs. Todd then completed four straight passes to take the Jets to the Buffalo 1, and fullback Kevin Long bulled it in to make it 31–27 with 3:44 left.

The Bills squandered their next possession and were forced to punt, giving the Jets a drive start at their own 20-yard line with 2:36 to go and two timeouts at their disposal. Todd's first-down throw to Shuler was good for 29 yards, and a 26-yard completion to Gaffney brought the ball to the Buffalo 25. The Bills stymied the Jets for two downs, bringing about a third-and-12 from the 27. Once again an apparent interception was nullified by a penalty. This time, Steve Freeman's would-be game saver was killed when Mario Clark was called for holding, and the Jets had yet another gift-wrapped opportunity. Todd's seven-yard pass to Scott Dierking moved the ball to the 11 and gave the Jets their 23rd first down of the game. Todd

then overthrew Shuler in the end zone, stopping the clock with 10 seconds remaining. On second down, Todd tried to force the ball in to Gaffney, about four yards deep in the end zone. Bill Simpson, who was responsible for covering Dierking out of the backfield, sniffed it out and made the play of the game—and the season—by intercepting Todd's pass at the 2 to stop the Jets from completing a miraculous comeback.

"I read Todd's eyes and saw he was coming to Gaffney," Simpson said. "I just stepped in front of him, and the ball was right there."

Simpson's last-second heroics secured Buffalo's first playoff win since 1965 and allowed the Bills to advance to the AFC Divisional Playoff Game against the Cincinnati Bengals the following week. But that's where the dream season came to an end, as the Bills fell to the eventual AFC champions.

Game Details

Buffalo Bills 31 • New York Jets 27

Bills	17	7	0	7	**31**
Jets	0	10	3	14	**27**

Date: December 27, 1981

Team Records: Bills 10–6, Jets 10–5–1

Scoring Plays:

BUF—TD Romes 26-yard fumble return (Mike-Mayer PAT)

BUF—TD Lewis 50-yard pass from Ferguson (Mike-Mayer PAT)

BUF—FG Mike-Mayer 29 yards

BUF—TD Lewis 26-yard pass from Fergruson (Mike-Mayer PAT)

NY—TD Shuler 30-yard pass from Todd (Leahy PAT)

NY—FG Leahy 26 yards

NY—FG Leahy 19 yards

BUF—TD Cribbs 45-yard run (Mike-Mayer PAT)

NY—TD B. Jones 30-yard pass from Todd (Leahy PAT)

NY—TD Long 1-yard run (Leahy PAT)

> **I** knew we were going to win, but I didn't know how.
>
> —BILLS DEFENSIVE END BEN WILLIAMS

Bill Simpson

One could say that Bill Simpson's interception against the New York Jets in the 1981 AFC Wild Card Game was an act of atonement. After all, it was just a year earlier in the AFC Divisional Playoff Game against the San Diego Chargers that the former Ram was beaten by wide receiver Ron Smith for the game-winning touchdown.

"People made more of that play than I ever did," Simpson said. "I made other mistakes and good plays in that game that people don't remember. But people remember the big plays at the end of a game, and I'm just glad they're going to be remembering this one instead of the other one."

Simpson is, of course, remembered for much more than just those two plays during his eight-year NFL career. A standout defensive back and punter at Michigan State, Simpson was drafted by the Los Angeles Rams in the second round in 1974. In five years with the Rams, he twice led the team in interceptions (1975 and 1977), was chosen All-Pro twice (1977 and 1978), and helped guide the team to the playoffs after each season.

He was acquired by the Bills in May 1979 in exchange for a draft choice, becoming one of several Rams who joined former head coach Chuck Knox after he took over the reins in Buffalo. (The others were kicker Tom Dempsey, linebacker Isiah Robertson, wide receiver Ron Jessie, and running back Lawrence McCutcheon.) After sitting out his first season in Buffalo as a result of injuries, Simpson stepped in as the team's starting free safety in 1980, replacing Tony Greene, and registered an interception in each of his first three games. In tandem with strong safety Steve Freeman, he became part of a formidable rear guard that was noted as much for its smarts as it was for its physicality. He enjoyed three solid seasons with the Bills, playing a major role in the team's playoff runs in 1980 and 1981.

The strike-shortened 1982 season might have been his best as a Bill, as the 6'1", 184-pound Detroit native led the club in tackles (65) and interceptions (4). It was also his last, however, as the injury-plagued Simpson announced his retirement in April 1983. He ended his career with 34 interceptions, 12 coming during his three years in Buffalo.

Simpson was inducted into the Archdiocese of Detroit Catholic High School Hall of Fame in 2007.

Safety Bill Simpson's second interception of the day sealed the victory over the New York Jets. *(Photo courtesy Getty Images/Robert L. Smith/NFL)*

November 25, 1965

Booker Doesn't Let Bambi Get Away

Edgerson Chases Down Speedy Alworth, Forces Fumble, Saves the Day

Long before Don Beebe became the enduring symbol of the never-quit spirit of the Buffalo Bills, there was Booker Edgerson. The spectacle of Beebe chasing down Leon Lett and swatting the ball from his hands to prevent another humiliating score in Buffalo's 52–17 loss to the Dallas Cowboys in Super Bowl XXVII brought to mind Edgerson's breathtaking chase-down of Lance Alworth in the Bills 20–20 tie with the San Diego Chargers at Balboa Stadium in November 1965. Players present to witness Edgerson's effort point to Beebe's memorable play as the only apt comparison.

According to Bills wide receiver Ed Rutkowski, Edgerson's play put the Chargers on notice that any inkling they had that the previous year's championship game was some sort of a fluke was little more than a delusion.

"Coming off the championship in '64, they felt they were still a better team and they were going to show us in '65," Rutkowski said. "We played a home game in '65,

and we couldn't get out of our own way and they beat us. Then we had an opportunity to go out there and play on the coast. We knew after that one play there was no way they were going to beat us again."

The Bills took the initial lead of the game in the first quarter when Jack Kemp tossed a six-yarder to Wray Carlton to make it 7–0. But the Chargers stormed back to take a 10–7 edge before the half. Buffalo regained the momentum early in the third quarter, with Kemp leading the offense on a 79-yard scoring drive that Daryle Lamonica finished off with a one-yard run to make it 14–10. The Chargers struck back on their next possession and appeared to be on the verge of reclaiming the lead in spectacular fashion when Edgerson stepped in to steal their thunder.

"We were in a zone," Edgerson remembered. "[Alworth] was out on my side, but he cut across the middle and was wide open."

"He ran a quick post and beat Booker by about two steps," Rutkowski said. "[Chargers signal-caller John] Hadl hit him with a perfect pass right in stride, and Lance was off to the races."

Chargers defensive tackle Ernie Ladd (77) assists on a tackle on Bills fullback Wray Carlton (30) on November 25, 1965. *(Photo courtesy Getty Images/Richard Stagg/NFL)*

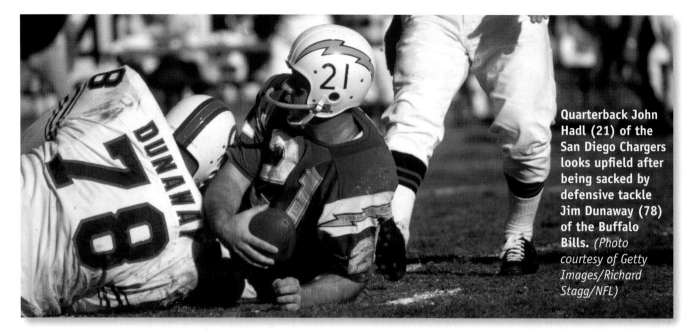

Quarterback John Hadl (21) of the San Diego Chargers looks upfield after being sacked by defensive tackle Jim Dunaway (78) of the Buffalo Bills. *(Photo courtesy of Getty Images/Richard Stagg/NFL)*

But Edgerson displayed his trademark indomitable spirit in doing what seemed to be the impossible—chasing down Alworth (nicknamed Bambi for his blazing speed) from behind after a 65-yard gallop and forcing him to fumble.

"I saw that there was no back coming out [and] no other receiver coming across, so I just took off after him and, fortunately, I caught him. Maybe he thought he was home free, but I know it shocked the hell out of him when I hit him."

"Here was a man who never got caught from behind," Rutkowski said. "He could outrun everything—like a deer. But Booker doesn't let up. He runs him down, catches him, and tackles him from behind at about the 15-yard line. Lance is still struggling, he's holding onto the ball, and right behind are [John] Tracey, [Mike] Stratton, and [Harry] Jacobs. [Alworth fumbled] and Tracey recovered in the end zone."

The play prevented the go-ahead touchdown and gave the Bills possession at their own 20. Moments later, Pete Gogolak extended the lead to 17–10 with a 12-yard chip shot. The Chargers came back in the fourth, however, taking a 20–17 lead on a Herb Travenio field goal and Paul Lowe's recovery of a fumble in the end zone for a touchdown at 8:37. A last-minute drive beginning at their own 25 stalled at the San Diego 15 with just six seconds left. Gogolak then nailed a 22-yarder, and Buffalo escaped with a 20–20 tie, thanks in no small part to Edgerson's touchdown-saving play.

Game Details

Buffalo Bills 20 • San Diego Chargers 20

Bills	7	0	10	3	**20**
Chargers	0	10	0	10	**20**

Date: November 25, 1965

Team Records: Bills 8–2, Chargers 6–2–2

Scoring Plays:

BUF—TD Carlton 6-yard pass from Kemp (Gogolak PAT)

SD—TD Lowe 6-yard run (Travenio PAT)

SD—FG Travenio 9 yards

BUF—TD Lamonica 1-yard run (Gogolak PAT)

BUF—FG Gogolak 12 yards

SD—FG Travenio 14 yards

SD—TD Lowe recovered fumble in end zone (Travenio PAT)

BUF—FG Gogolak 22 yards

"It was the defining moment of the game, maybe even the season," Rutkowski said. "You could see their sideline whooping, and then all of a sudden we recovered it in the end zone. It was, 'What happened?' They gave us their best shot, and we gave it right back to them."

It was a tone-setter. The two teams would meet again at the same site a month later for the rematch of the '64 title game. This time, the outcome would be even more decisive, as the Bills laid a 23–0 shellacking on the Chargers to claim their second straight AFL crown.

Booker Edgerson

It was sort of like a homecoming for Booker Edgerson when he signed a free agent contract with the Buffalo Bills in 1962. After all, Edgerson had played his college ball at Western Illinois University under Lou Saban, Joel Collier, and Red Miller, who made up three-fifths of the Buffalo coaching staff in 1962. When the AFL started two years earlier, the trio was hired as part of the first staff of the Boston Patriots. But by the time Edgerson graduated from Western Illinois and could make his way east to New England, Saban and his staff had been fired. "Fortunately, [Saban] ended up with the Bills," Edgerson said. "He called me and I said, 'Send me a contract.' So I signed with the Bills. It all worked out great."

Edgerson spent eight seasons with the Bills and recorded 23 interceptions in that time. In addition to his duties as a member of one of the best defensive secondaries in the league, Edgerson acted like a player-coach on the field. "Booker was my player-mentor," remembered Edgerson's companion corner, Butch Byrd, who came to the Bills in 1964. "We would get together before games, and he would tell me about different quarterbacks' strategies and tendencies [and] wide receivers' strategies and tendencies, because this was the first time I was facing them."

Edgerson used his natural leadership skills in his post-football life as well, helping shape the future of

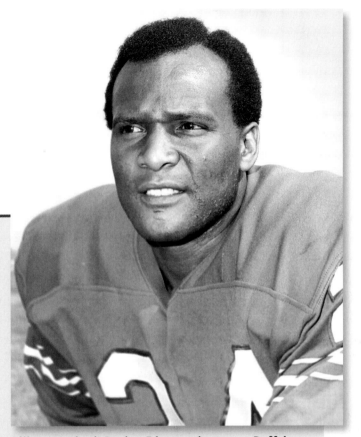

Bills cornerback Booker Edgerson became a Buffalo legend in November 1965 when he ran down Chargers speedster Lance Rentzel and stripped the ball away, preventing a touchdown. Edgerson was a stalwart in the Bills secondary for eight seasons. *(Photo courtesy Robert L. Smith, Orchard Park, NY)*

thousands of individuals at Erie Community College in Buffalo, where he served as the director of equity and diversity from 1982 until his retirement in 2007. In 1993, he was presented with the Ralph C. Wilson Jr. Distinguished Service Award, given to former Bills players for outstanding service to the organization and the community. Though he never went to an All-Star game and only received one All-AFL mention (1969), Edgerson was honored for his standout career with the Bills when he was inducted into the Greater Buffalo Sports Hall of Fame in 2001. He is also enshrined in the Western Illinois Athletics Hall of Fame (class of 1996).

September 12, 1993

Darby Pick Closes Door on 'Boys Comeback

Matt Darby's Late Interception Ices Buffalo Victory Over Cowboys

The Buffalo Bills opened the 1993 season with an impressive 38–14 victory over the New England Patriots. One week later we traveled to Dallas to do battle with the Cowboys, the team against whom we had humiliated ourselves by committing nine turnovers in the course of losing the previous season's Super Bowl by a score of 52–17. Without a doubt in my mind, it had been those turnovers that were responsible for the rout we suffered on that dismal evening in Pasadena. In that game, we had gained 362 yards from scrimmage, so if you don't count the five fumbles we lost and the four interceptions we threw, you might say we had a pretty good day on offense. Yeah, sure.

Now in our early-season rematch, it would once again be turnovers, not other statistics, that would prove to be most meaningful. In this game the Cowboys outgained us 393 yards to our feeble 229, but the impact of those exchanges of possession was felt even more profoundly because of an often-overlooked aspect of the turnover battle. It was something I had drummed at our players relentlessly: "It is what you do after a takeaway or a giveaway occurs that really matters." On offense, do you capitalize on it? On defense, do you whimper about how your teammates screwed up, or do you go out there and meet the challenge with resolve? In no game during my 47-year coaching career have I ever seen a team respond as effectively as our Buffalo Bills did on that late summer afternoon in Dallas.

On the Cowboys' first possession, cornerback Nate Odomes intercepted a Troy Aikman pass intended for Michael Irvin, and our offense did something about it. Jim Kelly capped off a 12-play, 63-yard touchdown drive by connecting on a 10-yard scoring pass to fullback Carwell Gardner, giving us a 7–0 lead.

Late in the first quarter, Kelly was sacked and stripped of the ball. Cowboys defensive tackle Russell Maryland recovered at our 43. Then it was our defense that did something about it. They forced a punt three plays later, but on the last play of the quarter, Dallas forced still another turnover by intercepting a pass at our 34. However, they were able to advance just three yards, and when their 49-yard field goal attempt went wide right, they remained scoreless despite having taken the ball away from us twice—and both times on our side of midfield—in the first period.

Midway into the second, it was our turn to play takeaway again. Linebacker Mark Maddox forced a fumble, which cornerback James Williams recovered at the Dallas 37. We didn't move the ball very well, but Steve Christie's 48-yard field goal allowed us to come away with some points. Just before the half ended, Dallas culminated a long drive by kicking a 42-yard field goal, and we went to the locker room with a 10–3 lead.

That's also what the score was at the end of three quarters of play, but as the fourth quarter began, Dallas started a drive at their own 2. Fourteen plays and more than seven

minutes later, they took it into our end zone from four yards out, and the score was tied at 10–10.

Matters appeared to be getting increasingly worse when we were unable to pick up a first down on our next possession, but our punt-coverage team helped things get better in a hurry. Mark Maddox forced his second fumble of the day, and then Steve Tasker recovered it at the Dallas 34. Thurman Thomas carried the ball five times and inched it down to the 17-yard line. Steve Christie then booted a 35-yarder that put us ahead 13–10.

There was still 2:43 remaining when Aikman & Co. began their last drive at their own 20, and they were effective. With just 12 seconds left, Dallas was at our 12 when Aikman threw a ball toward the end zone that was intended for tight end Jay Novacek. Novacek had already caught eight passes for 106 yards, but he didn't get to catch this

Matt Darby (43) celebrates his interception of Cowboys quarterback Troy Aikman. *(Photo courtesy Getty Images/Tim Roberts/AFP)*

Matt Darby

Safety Matt Darby was a four-year starter at UCLA before being selected by the Buffalo Bills in the fifth round of the 1992 draft. We had already taken linebacker Keith Goganious from Penn State in the third round. Little did we know that they had been close friends and high school teammates in Virginia Beach, Virginia—hometown of their new teammate Bruce Smith. Coincidences do occur.

Darby rode the wave of success the Bills were enjoying during his first two seasons, serving as a reserve safety and special teamer as the club returned for their third and fourth consecutive Super Bowls. The 6'2" 200-pounder earned a starting role in 1994 when incumbent free safety Mark Kelso was hurt and had to go on injured reserve. Darby stepped in and enjoyed a fine season as he registered a team-best four interceptions. His promising career in Buffalo was cut short after an injury-plagued season in 1995 that saw him appear is just seven games. Darby was released by the club during the off-season but subsequently signed with the Arizona Cardinals, where he spent his two final NFL seasons.

In retirement, Darby put his training and skills as a finely tuned athlete to good use, becoming a certified strength and conditioning specialist and personal trainer. In 2006, he founded Play2Win, a Florida-based public speaking firm that trains athletes to learn how to be successful on and off the field.

one. Our nickel back, Matt Darby, leapt in front of him and snared it at our 1-yard line. Wisely, he went to the ground immediately. Time expired two plays later, and the Buffalo Bills were victorious.

In that game we had turned over the ball twice in our own territory. On both occasions our defense—led that day by Darryl Talley's 12 tackles—rose to the challenge and kept the Cowboys from scoring any points. Our defense was also responsible for taking the ball away from the Cowboys four times during Revenge Afternoon, and our offense played well enough to convert three of those takeaways into the 13 points we needed to win that closely fought contest.

> That was my biggest play, for sure, in pro, college, high school, whatever. The ball got popped in the air, and luckily I found it and I got a chance to dive for it. I didn't know they were going to Novacek, but I had a pretty good idea.
>
> **—BILLS SAFETY MATT DARBY**

The Buffalo Bills drafted safety Matt Darby in the fifth round in 1992.
(Photo courtesy of Getty Images)

Game Details

Buffalo Bills 13 • Dallas Cowboys 10

Bills	7	3	0	3	**13**
Cowboys	0	3	0	7	**10**

Date: September 12, 1993

Team Records: Bills 1–0, Cowboys 0–1

Scoring Plays:

BUF—TD Gardner 10-yard pass from Kelly (Christie PAT)

BUF—FG Christie 48 yards

DAL—FG Elliott 43 yards

BUF—TD Williams 5-yard run (Elliott PAT)

BUF—FG Christie 35 yards

September 7, 2003

Adams Rumbles

Sam Adams Returns Brady Pass for a Score in Dramatic Season-Opening Triumph

Like so many other season openers the Buffalo Bills had played, the one scheduled to kick off the 2003 season was seen as a new beginning. After all, the team had busied itself during the offseason with bringing in established veterans who could make an immediate impact on the defensive side of the ball, an area in which some observers felt the team had been sorely deficient. To that end, the Bills signed three of the most sought-after free agents on the market in defensive tackle Sam Adams and linebackers Takeo Spikes and Jeff Posey. But in what might be one of the most heralded acquisitions in team history, the Bills landed All-Pro safety Lawyer Milloy—who had just been released by the New England Patriots for salary cap reasons—four days before the Bills were scheduled to start the season against those very same Patriots.

Add to the Milloy signing the fact that Bills quarterback Drew Bledsoe was also just two years earlier a member of the Patriots, and all of a sudden the season opener had taken on a whole new meaning.

The new-look Bills established themselves early and emphatically, building a 14–0 lead by the early second quarter on a one-yard touchdown run by Travis Henry and a seven-yard Bledsoe pass to tight end Dave Moore. It was now time for the defense to get in on the fun. Tom Brady, the man who had taken Bledsoe's place as the starting signal-caller for the Patriots in 2001 (and had subsequently led them to victory in Super Bowl XXXVI) had the Pats on the move at his own 37. He dropped back to pass and attempted to throw, but the ball was tipped into the air. It came down and nestled in the bosom of Sam Adams, the Bills new defensive tackle. Adams took hold and immediately shifted into his highest gear. Accompanied by a convoy of blockers that included linebackers Posey and Spikes, Adams made his way toward the sideline and rumbled all the way to the end zone for the score and a 21–0 Buffalo lead.

"That's how we wanted to execute it," said Adams as he explained the defensive scheme that resulted in the turnover. "The way it worked, I was able to come around in the passing lane, and then I got escorted down the line."

Adams' touchdown would not be the only statement made by the defense during that first half. The rejuvenated unit held Brady and the vaunted Patriots to a measly 51 yards and six first downs—and two of those had been the result of penalties.

Unfortunately for New England fans, there was more misery in store in the second half as the Bills scored 10 fourth-quarter points on a Travis Henry 9-yard run and a Rian Lindell field goal to secure a 31–0 thrashing of the mighty Patriots.

The Bills had held Brady & Co. to 239 total offensive yards, while limiting Brady himself to 123 in the air and forcing four interceptions in handing the Patriots their first shutout loss in 10 years. The newcomers figured prominently in the win, with Adams' big play and Spikes picking off two passes and recording six tackles. Lawyer Milloy recorded a sack and five tackles, plus he deflected a pass that turned into an interception for Nate Clements.

Drew Bledsoe, the other ex-Patriot involved, finished 17-of-28 for 230 yards and a touchdown. After the game, Patriots head coach Bill Belichick refused to be baited into acknowledging the role that Bledsoe and Milloy had played in the Bills victory, saying simply, "We didn't play well."

Unfortunately for the Bills, this game would stand as the high point of the season. The

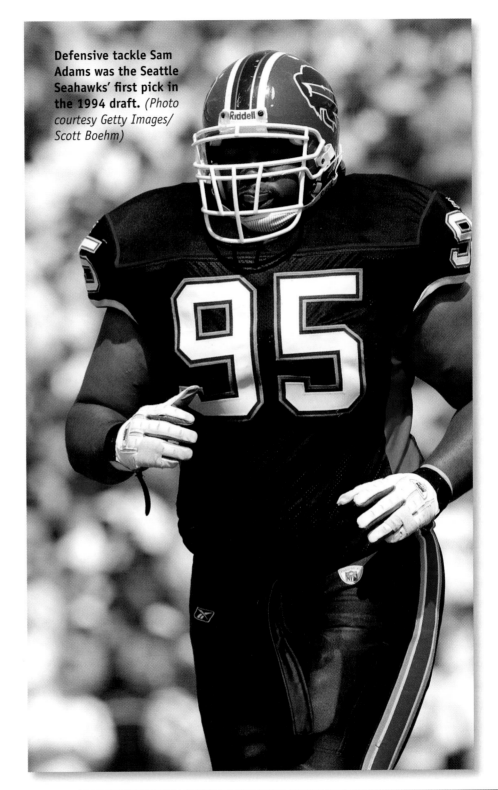

Defensive tackle Sam Adams was the Seattle Seahawks' first pick in the 1994 draft. *(Photo courtesy Getty Images/ Scott Boehm)*

team failed to live up to its potential and limped to a disappointing 6–10 record that led to the firing of head coach Gregg Williams. The Patriots, on the other hand, turned their season around and wound up in the Super Bowl for the second time in three seasons. In one of the most ironic twists in the annals of pro football, the Patriots turned the tables when the clubs met again for the season finale in Foxboro on December 27, laying a 31–0 shellacking on the Bills to bring an ignominious end to a season that had begun so promisingly.

> **I**'m glad he got the touchdown. He was moving away from the offensive linemen. But you know what? I can get him in the 40.
>
> —BILLS OFFENSIVE TACKLE MIKE WILLIAMS

Game Details

Buffalo Bills 31 • New England Patriots 0

Patriots	0	0	0	0	**0**
Bills	7	14	0	10	**31**

Date: September 7, 2003

Team Records: Bills 0–0, Patriots 0–0

Scoring Plays:

BUF—TD Henry 1-yard run (Lindell PAT)

BUF—TD Moore 7-yard pass from Bledsoe (Lindell PAT)

BUF—TD Adams 37-yard interception return (Lindell PAT)

BUF—TD Henry 9-yard run (Lindell PAT)

BUF—FG Lindell 44 yards

Drew Bledsoe entered Gillette Stadium as an opposing quarterback for the first time on December 8, 2002. (*Photo courtesy AP Images*)

Sam Adams

Sam Adams was already a nine-year veteran by the time he signed with the Bills as a free agent in 2003, having spent six years with the Seattle Seahawks, two with the Baltimore Ravens, and one with the Oakland Raiders. The 6'4", 335-pound defensive tackle was the Seahawks first-round pick in the 1994 draft (eighth overall) after a standout career at Texas A&M in which he was a consensus All-American in his junior and final season. During his time in Seattle, "Man Mountain," so-called by his teammates, developed into one of the premier defensive linemen in the game, and he was chosen as an alternate for the 1997 Pro Bowl.

Adams signed with the Baltimore Ravens prior to the 2000 season and received his first Pro Bowl nod that year for his huge role in the success of the Ravens' defense, which ranked first overall and keyed the team's victory over the Giants in Super Bowl XXXV. Another Pro Bowl appearance followed the 2001 season, and Adams' market value skyrocketed. He signed with the Oakland Raiders in 2002 and made a return trip the big game, but the Raiders lost to the Tampa Bay Buccaneers in Super Bowl XXXVII.

The Bills signed Adams in March 2003, and the big man had an immediate impact, making the play described above in his first start and becoming a dominant force in the interior of the team's defense. His outstanding play earned him a third trip to the Pro Bowl in 2004 and helped the Bills defense rank second in the league that year. But Adams became a victim of football economics following the 2006 season when the Bills were forced to release the 12-year veteran in order to make room under the salary cap. He played one season with the Cincinnati Bengals before moving on to the Denver Broncos for a 14th and ultimately final season in 2007.

In addition to his participation in the game on the field, Adams involved himself in the management end when he became an owner of the Everett (Washington) Hawks of the National Indoor Football League in 2004. Two years later, Adams moved the Hawks to a new league, Arena Football 2. Failing financially, the team folded after the 2007 season.

Adams' father, Sam Sr., had an outstanding 10-year career in the NFL as an offensive guard with the New England Patriots (1972–80) and New Orleans Saints (1981).

Sam Adams (95) of the Buffalo Bills runs back his interception for a touchdown against the New England Patriots. *(Photo courtesy Getty Images/Rick Stewart)*

November 8, 1987

Cornelius Comes to Town

Cornelius Bennett's First NFL Sack Stops Denver Comeback

I still recall Cornelius Bennett's first game in the NFL. I'm sure John Elway remembers it, too.

The Denver Broncos came to town on November 8, 1987. Earlier that week, Bills general manager Bill Polian had negotiated the trade that brought Bennett, the year's overall No. 1 draft choice who was still unsigned by the Indianapolis Colts, to Buffalo. Bennett wasn't ready to start when his first Sunday with the team arrived, but we determined that once the game was underway, we would send in "Biscuit" (the nickname by which—I don't know why—he came to be known) for a play or two so his initiation to the big time might begin.

Late in the first quarter of what was then a scoreless game, Denver had the ball, third-and-6 at their own 24. We sent in Bennett as part of our pass-rush package. Elway dropped back to pass, and when he saw what was streaking at him from off of our left side, he unloaded the ball just as No. 55 (in subsequent years his number was changed to No. 97) blasted him to the turf. I recall seeing Elway pick himself up and glance at Bennett with one of those "Who is this guy?" looks. The pass was incomplete and, after the Broncos punted, we took over in favorable

field position as the second quarter began. From there, Jim Kelly engineered a 10-play drive that culminated with a 9-yard scoring pass to Andre Reed, and we led 7–0.

Our defense was alive now, bringing constant hurries on Elway. The first came from Darryl Talley on first-and-10 at their 17, then another came from Bruce Smith on second-and-10. On third-and-10, we sent that rookie Bennett back onto the field, and he did it again. With the fastest head-nod and sidestep I'd ever seen by a linebacker, Bennett whistled past Elway's protectors and forced another incompletion.

The Broncos punted, but this time we didn't get the ball in favorable field position. Instead, Robb Riddick blocked Mike Horan's kick, and the ball went bounding out the back of the end zone for a safety, giving us a 9–0 lead. Riddick's special-team heroics were only part of the big contribution he made in this game. In addition, he was our leading ground gainer with 78 yards on 19 carries, including one he took in for a touchdown.

Throughout the remainder of the first half, our pressure on Elway remained intense. When he tried to scramble, our other rookie linebacker Shane Conlan was there to make the tackle. Conlan led the team with seven

Buffalo Bills linebacker Cornelius Bennett.
(Photo courtesy AP Images/Charles Agel)

tackles, three of them made in bringing down the fleet-footed Denver quarterback.

Late in the second quarter, we put together another 10-play touchdown drive, this one beginning at our own 25. Riddick's one-yard plunge topped it off, and with just less than a minute remaining in the half, we were in front 16–0. Denver tried to retaliate, but with only seven seconds left they had to punt it away from their own 23. This time it was master punt-blocker Steve Tasker who replicated Riddick's earlier feat. Tasker blocked Horan's punt, and this one also exited the back of the end zone for a safety. At halftime we led 18–0, and things were looking pretty darn good. But don't celebrate yet, Bills fans!

We started the second half rather well. Scott Norwood nailed a 30-yard field goal to give us a 21–0 lead. For Denver, the first half had been a disaster. Elway had completed just one of his nine pass attempts, mostly because of the pass-rush heat that he had to deal with. They were also zero-for-seven in third-down efficiency. We had outgained them 280 yards to 60, plus we had blocked two punts, both of which resulted in safeties. Apparently Dan Reeves and the Denver coaching staff made some superb halftime adjustments, because after Norwood's field goal, the Broncos were a different team from the one we had seen during the first half.

Starting their next series at their own 28, Elway hit wide receiver Vance Johnson for gains of 15 and 51 yards, followed immediately by Sammy Winder's 5-yard touchdown run. Three plays, 72 yards, seven points. It was 21–7 as the third quarter ended.

Three minutes into the fourth, the Broncos began a drive at their own 10. Now it was John Elway at his best.

He took his team the full distance on a 15-play march that took more than nine minutes off the clock. Along the way, he converted three third-down situations and completed eight of his last nine passes, the final one being a 15-yard strike to Johnson. It was now an uncomfortable 21–14 score.

We ate some time off the clock by running the ball, but late in the game we were forced to punt, and Denver's offense had one final opportunity to score the touchdown that could tie it up. We sent our pass-rush unit onto the field and, while taking a deep breath, I included Cornelius Bennett in that group. We knew he was going to try to rush the passer. They knew he was going to try to rush the passer. The whole world knew he was going to try to rush the passer. And guess what? He rushed the passer. Bennett got back there as quickly as Elway did and got his very first sack as an NFL player. (It wouldn't be his last.) On second-and-18, Bennett brought the pressure again and forced an incompletion. Victory was assured. Bills 21, Broncos 14.

Game Details

Buffalo Bills 21 • Denver Broncos 14

Broncos	0	0	7	7	**14**
Bills	0	18	3	0	**21**

Date: November 8, 1987

Team Records: Bills 4–3, Broncos 4–2–1

Scoring Plays:

BUF—TD Reed 9-yard pass from Kelly (Norwood PAT)

BUF—Safety Riddick blocked punt out of end zone

BUF—TD Riddick 1-yard run (Norwood PAT)

BUF—Safety Tasker blocked punt out of end zone

BUF—FG Norwood 30 yards

DEN—TD Winder 6-yard run (Karlis PAT)

DEN—TD V. Johnson 15-yard pass from Elway (Karlis PAT)

> **B**iscuit had a sack, two quarterback pressures, and three tackles in limited action that day. He totally transformed our defense.
>
> —BILLS SPECIAL TEAMER STEVE TASKER

Cornelius Bennett

The Buffalo Bills entered the 1987 draft intent on strengthening our defense. Apparently, the Indianapolis Colts, who had the first pick in the entire draft, were of the same mind. They selected the top-rated player on almost everyone's draft board when they went for linebacker Cornelius Bennett from the University of Alabama. We didn't get to pick until the eighth spot, but we were beside ourselves with glee when another linebacker, Shane Conlan from Penn State, was still available. We picked him, and we were rewarded immediately as Conlan showed he was going to be a starter right away. Halfway into his rookie season he was already playing at a level that surpassed even what we had anticipated.

On a Monday, seven games into that 1987 season, general manager Bill Polian peeked into my office and asked if I'd like to add Cornelius Bennett to our roster. "You're kidding," I said. I knew the Colts and Bennett had been unable to agree on contract terms and that he was still back home in Alabama, but I couldn't fathom that they would be open to trading away his rights, especially to a team in their division.

"Not kidding," Polian countered. "I've been talking with them and the L.A. Rams on a three-way deal that would involve that great running back, Eric Dickerson, going from the Rams to Indy while Bennett would come to us."

"Sounds great," I said. "What do we have to give up?"

"We'd send Greg Bell (the Bills' first-round choice in the 1984 draft), our first-round pick in the 1988 draft, plus our first- and second-round picks in the 1989 draft to the Rams," he told me.

After I regained consciousness, I was able to blurt out, "No way! Are you crazy? Two firsts, a second, and a top-flight running back for some guy who's never played a down of pro football?"

Six hours later, after being subjected to the rationale of Polian, the most persuasive individual to ever sit in an NFL office, I succumbed to his logic. Boy, am I glad I did.

One magnificent by-product of the trade for Bennett came less than a year later when—during the draft prior to the 1988 season—we found ourselves without the first-round choice we had sent to the Rams. This time we wanted to pick a top-flight running back, but by the time we got to make our first pick it was well into the second round, and seven running backs had already been plucked off of the board. As a result, we had to settle for some fellow named Thurman Thomas. If you want to see what he looks like, all you have to do is go to the Pro Football Hall of Fame in Canton, Ohio. I hear there is a bust of him on display there.

Cornelius Bennett terrorized NFL quarterbacks during his career.
(Photo courtesy AP Images)

December 9, 1990

Bruuuce is Looose!

The Great Bruce Smith Registers Four Sacks to Lead the Bills to Victory

Few things energized Rich Stadium crowds like the sight of Bruce Smith laying waste to enemy quarterbacks. In fact, he recorded so many (171) in his 15 years with the Bills that the quarterback sack and Bruce Smith became synonymous. Since it would be nearly impossible to pick just one sack to focus on, let's extend the playbook and focus our attention instead on the four sacks he had in a single game against Indianapolis in 1990 and the role they played in our victory that day.

Our opening game of that season had been at home against the Colts, the very day we first unveiled the No-Huddle Offense that was to become emblematic of the Buffalo Bills during the first half of the 1990s. In that meeting at Rich Stadium, fans were dazzled by our unique offensive exploits but now, three months later, we were at Indianapolis, and this time it was the performance of our defense that stole the show.

It was really no contest right from the get-go. On our first possession, our No-Huddle Maniacs cruised 66 yards in six plays, finishing it off with a 34-yard scoring strike from Jim Kelly to Andre Reed. Then the Colts took over—

sort of. They got as far as their own 42, and that's where our cornerback Kirby Jackson picked off a Jeff George pass and brought it back to their 37. Four plays later it was once again Kelly to Reed for a seven-yard touchdown. Bills 14, Colts 0.

The Colts began their next series at their own 20. Eric Dickerson started things off with a two-yard pickup on first down. On second, Bruce Smith sacked Jeff George for a loss of six yards. On third down, Smith sacked George again—this time for a loss of 13 yards—and the Colts were forced to punt. We started at their 40-yard line, and four plays later we were at their 8. On the next play we fumbled it away—our only giveaway of the game—and the Colts got it out to their 25-yard line as the first quarter ended.

On the first play of the second quarter, guess what? Smith sacked George for a loss of seven yards. On second-and-17, strong safety John Hagy intercepted George's pass, and although our drive ended with Rick "Bootin" Tuten's first punt of the contest, George couldn't have been too happy about going back onto the field and having to see old No. 78 take his place across the line of scrimmage. George had good reason not to be elated. Four plays into a modest drive on a first-and-10 situation, Smith did it again—sack number four for another seven-yard loss. Indy punted. We took over on our own 36 and 11 plays later, Thurman Thomas scored on a 5-yard run. We were in command now by a score of 21–0. On the next series, George was sacked once again, but the remarkable thing about it was that this time it wasn't Bruce Smith. It was cornerback Clifford Hicks who, on a blitz, came flying in unimpeded as the Colts assigned three (at least) of their pass protectors to blocking No. 78.

When the second half began, the Colts finally did get something going, and they marched 55 yards to a touchdown on nine plays. To George's credit, despite the tremendous pressure he had been under, he completed all four of his short-pass attempts on that drive. And it was George, on a sneak from the 1, who took it in for the score. When we got the ball back, Jim Kelly teamed up with Thomas on a 63-yard short-pass/long-run-after-the-catch play that put us in position for a 25-yard field goal by Scott

Defensive end Bruce Smith.
(Photo courtesy Getty Images/ George Rose)

Bruce Smith played for the Buffalo Bills from 1985–99. *(Photo courtesy Getty Images)*

Norwood, giving us a 24–7 lead. Just as the third quarter was ending, Clifford Hicks came on another corner blitz, and although he didn't get a sack this time, he tipped the pass as it was leaving George's hand and our other defensive end, Leon Seals, intercepted at midfield. We got it down to their 23, and from there Thomas scampered in for another Buffalo touchdown.

After that we just milked the clock, and the Colts were unable to move it at all. Our no-huddle offense had been as efficient as ever, but what a day it had been for our defense! The Colts had gained a total of just 127 yards on the day, and they had net passing yardage of a mere 52 yards. We had racked up five sacks (four of them by you-know-who), and we had picked off three passes. Smith, of course, had a banner day, but the pass pressure came from many others on the team, as well. Clifford Hicks, a defensive back, contributed a lot of that, and even though Smith's mates up front—Leon Seals and Jeff Wright—hadn't registered any sacks, they also had brought consistent pressure to bear on Jeff George. Final score: Bills 31, Colts 7.

Game Details

Buffalo Bills 31 • Indianapolis Colts 7

Bills	14	7	3	7	**31**
Colts	0	0	7	0	**7**

Date: December 9, 1990
Team Records: Bills 10–2, Colts 5–7
Scoring Plays:
BUF—TD Reed 34-yard pass from Kelly (Norwood PAT)
BUF—TD Reed 7-yard pass from Kelly (Norwood PAT)
BUF—TD Thomas 5-yard run (Norwood PAT)
IND—TD George 1-yard run (Biasucci PAT)
BUF—FG Norwood 25 yards
BUF—TD Thomas 23-yard run (Norwood PAT)

Bruuuce!

The Bills-Colts game of December 9, 1990, was not the only time during his career that Bruce Smith sacked the opposing team's quarterbacks four times. He repeated that performance four years later in a game against the Houston Oilers. The only other Buffalo Bills player to record four sacks in one game was Cornelius Bennett who did it against the Philadelphia Eagles during his rookie season in 1987.

During the 1990 season, Bruce Smith sacked opposing quarterbacks a total of 19 times, the highest number he attained in any year during his illustrious Hall of Fame career. During 12 of the 15 years that Smith played for the Bills, his sack figures were in double numbers. As a Bills player, Smith sacked opposing quarterbacks 171 times. He added 29 more in his final NFL years as a member of the Washington Redskins, making him the only player in the game's history with 200 career sacks. And aside from all that, the man was great against the run.

During the Bills' Super Bowl era and even beyond, Smith was the most intimidating defensive player in the NFL. Even Lawrence Taylor, perhaps the greatest linebacker who ever lived and the man who personified intimidation prior to Smith's emergence, conceded as much prior to the Bills-Giants meeting in Super Bowl XXV. Anthony Munoz, the greatest offensive tackle of the era, summed up the prospect of playing against Smith in one word: "Scary."

The Virginia Tech All-American was the first player selected in the 1985 NFL draft. The 6'4", 280-pound defensive end had turned around the football program at Virginia Tech and was expected to do the same for the floundering Bills, who had suffered through a miserable 2–14 season in 1984. Man, did he ever live up to expectations! After struggling early in his

I think he was a little rattled. If you get constant pressure on any quarterback, he's going to wonder where it's coming from. On one play, he saw me coming and he said, 'Oh, shit!' [Colts center] Ray Donaldson told me after the game they were supposed to double me on their blocking schemes. They got kind of confused, and by the time the second guy got over, it was too late. I was already back there.

—BILLS DEFENSIVE END BRUCE SMITH

rookie season, Smith rebounded to record six-and-a-half sacks and was named the AFC Defensive Rookie of the Year by the NFL Players Association, the first of literally hundreds of laurels he would garner over his 15 years in Buffalo. During that time, Smith made 11 trips to the Pro Bowl, was named All-Pro 12 times, earned recognition as NFL Defensive Player of the Year twice (1990 and 1996), and was named AFC Defensive Player of the Year four times (1987, 1988, 1990, and 1996).

Smith signed with the Washington Redskins after the 1999 season and played four more years before retiring as the league's all-time leading quarterback sacker, surpassing long-time rival Reggie White by two (200 to 198). When he retired after the 2003 season, Smith had played in a total of 279 games in his 19 years in the league. How appropriate it was that this great defensive end was selected to the Pro Football Hall of Fame in 2009, his first year of eligibility.

Special Teams Heroics

January 3, 1993

The Comeback

Christie's Overtime Field Goal Caps the Greatest Comeback in NFL History

On a dreary winter day in Orchard Park, the Buffalo Bills and the Houston Oilers met in the AFC Wild Card Playoff Game at Rich Stadium. In the season finale played just one week earlier, the Oilers had defeated the Bills by a score of 27–3. That loss had cost us the Eastern Division title and a first-round bye. We had been forced to play the game without the services of star quarterback Jim Kelly and All-Pro linebacker Cornelius Bennett, both of whom were injured and unable to play. Neither had recovered in time for the playoff game, and once again they would have to watch from the sideline. Compounding our problem was the fact that running back Thurman Thomas entered the game in dubious condition. He tried to play, but it was apparent that he was so limited that it was unwise to keep him on the field. Kenny Davis replaced Thurman, defensive back Kurt Schulz took over for Cornelius, and Frank Reich started in Kelly's place.

By halftime, matters were even worse than they had been the week before. The Oilers, led by quarterback Warren Moon, had scored on all four of their possessions in the first half. Moon had completed 19 of his 22 passes, four of them for touchdowns. The Oilers had gained 284 yards while limiting us to just 79. The score at intermission was Houston 28, Buffalo 3.

In the somber locker room, I did not resort to any pep-talk theatrics. All I recall saying was, "You are two-time defending AFC champions. When you walk off the field 30 minutes from now, don't let anyone be able to say you quit, that you gave up." Then I walked over to Frank Reich and said, "Frank, I understand that you led the greatest comeback in collegiate football history. Today you are going to lead the greatest comeback in NFL history." Reich didn't say anything. He merely nodded his head.

The Bills received the kickoff in the second half, and we began our drive at our own 36. Frank's pass on third-and-9 bounced off the hands of tight end Keith McKeller and into the arms of Houston defensive back Brian McDowell, who then raced 58 yards for yet another Houston touchdown. Less than two minutes into the second half, the score was now Houston 35, Buffalo 3.

The ensuing kickoff was flubbed, but we caught our first break of the game when the ball bounced off the chest of Mark Maddox—stationed in the front line of our return unit—who then recovered to give us possession at midfield. A 24-yard pass to Pete Metzelaars, a 16-yarder to Andre Reed, and four running plays by Kenny Davis resulted in the Bills' first touchdown when Davis hammered it in from one yard out. The score was now 35–10. Big deal!

Next, I instructed Steve Christie to go for it with an onside kick. Christie not only executed it perfectly, but he was the one to recover it, as well. Three plays later, Reich hit Don Beebe on a 38-yard touchdown strike. The score was 35–17.

Now it was time for the Buffalo defense to come to life. We forced Houston into a three-and-out and, as a result, we began our next drive at our own 41. Reich to James Lofton for 18 yards. Screen pass to Kenny Davis for 19 more. Reich to Reed for 26 yards and a touchdown, making it 35–24. This was starting to get sorta interesting.

Now it was the kickoff coverage unit that stepped up by forcing the Oilers to start their next possession at their own 15. On Houston's first play, strong safety Henry Jones

Buffalo Bills kicker Steve Christie kicks a 32-yard field goal with 11:54 left in overtime to give the Bills a 41–38 victory over the Houston Oilers. *(Photo courtesy Getty Images/Chuck Soloman/NFL)*

Buffalo Bills kicker Steve Christie (2) and quarterback Frank Reich (14) celebrate the 32-yard game-winning field goal. *(Photo courtesy Getty Images/ John H. Reid)*

picked off a pass at the Oilers 38, returning it to the 23. On fourth-and-5 at the 18, we called our first timeout of the half. A successful field goal would bring us within eight points. As we conferred along the sideline, however, Reich convinced me that he had the play that would work. "Go for it," I told him, while the pundits slapped their foreheads with the heels of their hands. Reich then drilled a pass over the middle to Andre Reed, who caught it at the 7-yard line and sprinted into the end zone. With the extra point, the score was now 35–31 as the quarter ended.

Once again, our Bills forced Houston to punt, but the Oilers stopped us, too, forcing us to punt it right back to them. There were 14 minutes to be played as the Oilers started a drive at their own 10. The drive lasted for 15 plays and ate up an excruciating seven-and-a-half minutes. They

reached the Buffalo 14, and the only reason they did not score a touchdown—one that would have given them an insurmountable 42–31 lead—was because of the most overlooked and perhaps the most crucial play of the day.

Houston had a second-and-10 at our 31, and it was there that Warren Moon made a play call that was perfectly selected and perfectly executed. It was a screen pass to his right to his outstanding running back, Lorenzo White. Bills defensive end Phil Hansen came rushing at Moon from Moon's right side, and as Hansen jumped in the air in an attempt to bat the pass, Houston's right tackle cut-blocked him. Hansen went spinning into the air and landed heavily on the ground.

In the meantime, Moon had delivered the pass to White who, with nothing between himself and the Buffalo goal line except his escort of three huge offensive linemen, set sail unimpeded toward the clinching touchdown. Without hesitating an instant after his jarring tumble, Hansen had sprung to his feet and, realizing that a screen-pass scenario was underway, had taken off in frantic chase of White. At the 20, Hansen dove desperately at White's heels and made just enough contact to cause White to stumble and go down. The Bills defense stiffened, and the Oilers had to settle for a field-goal attempt instead. The snap was fumbled, and we took over on our own 26 with six minutes left but still trailing 35–31.

There were four minutes remaining when the Bills faced a third-and-4 on our own 32. I told offensive coordinator Jim Shofner that we would be using all four downs. Knowing that, he called for a run instead of a pass. Kenny Davis broke it for a 35-yard gain, and four plays later it was once again a Frank Reich-to-Andre Reed pass good for 17 yards and a touchdown. Miraculously, we had taken the lead, 38–35, but there were still three minutes left to be played.

The thrills were a long way from being over. Moon engineered yet another long drive—13 plays—and reached our 9-yard line on fourth-and-3. With just 15 seconds in regulation, Al Del Greco's 26-yard field goal tied the score at 38 apiece. We were going into overtime.

> I was pretty emotional when I got back to the locker room. I couldn't hold back the tears. Without question it's the greatest game of my life. Your thought is to take it one play at a time and don't try to force anything. In thinking back to the experience in college, it wasn't any great thing that I did. We only threw 15 times in the second half of that game and we were down 31–0, so I knew it could be done. I never really thought, 'Oh, we're out of it.'
>
> —BILLS QUARTERBACK FRANK REICH

The Oilers won the toss and elected to receive. On their third play, Bills cornerback Nate Odomes intercepted, and three plays later Steve Christie booted a 32-yard field goal that won the game for the Bills. It was the greatest comeback in the history of the NFL.

When the postgame locker room celebration finally settled down, Frank Reich bounded up to me and said, "Coach, when you told me at halftime that I would lead the greatest comeback in NFL history, we were only down by 25 points. The greatest previous comeback was from a 28-point deficit. That's why I threw that interception for a Houston touchdown on the first series of the second half."

My response? "You know what, Frank? I'm going to tell you an even bigger lie. I believe you."

Game Details

Buffalo Bills 41 • Houston Oilers 38 (OT)

Oilers	7	21	7	3	0	**38**
Bills	3	0	28	7	3	**41**

Date: January 3, 1993

Team Records: Bills 11–5, Oilers 10–6

Scoring Plays:

HOU—TD Jeffires 3-yard pass from Moon (Del Greco PAT)

BUF—FG Christie 36 yards

HOU—TD Slaughter 7-yard pass from Moon (Del Greco PAT)

HOU—TD Duncan 26-yard pass from Moon (Del Greco PAT)

HOU—TD Jeffires 27-yard pass from Moon (Del Greco PAT)

HOU—TD McDowell 58-yard interception return (Del Greco PAT)

BUF—TD K. Davis 1-yard run (Christie PAT)

BUF—TD Beebe 38-yard pass from Reich (Christie PAT)

BUF—TD Reed 26-yard pass from Reich (Christie PAT)

BUF—TD Reed 18-yard pass from Reich (Christie PAT)

BUF—TD Reed 17-yard pass from Reich (Christie kick)

HOU—FG Del Greco 26 yards

BUF—FG Christie 32 yards in overtime

January 27, 1991

Wide Right

Norwood's 47-Yarder Sails Wide; Bills Lose in First Trip to Super Bowl

With 1:16 remaining in Super Bowl XXV, the New York Giants, leading 20–19 and facing a fourth-and-2 at the Buffalo 48, were forced to punt, giving the Bills possession at our own 10. One minute and eight seconds later, we had moved to their 29 on a drive that included Thurman Thomas runs of 11 and 22 yards. Thurman had carried 15 times during the game for 135 yards (an average of 9.0 per carry). To that he added 55 yards in pass receptions. Had the Bills emerged victorious, there is little doubt Thurman would have been the game's MVP.

Twice during the regular season—a 29–28 win against Denver and a 30–27 victory over the Jets—kicker Scott Norwood had provided the field goals that represented the winning points. He made the other field goal he had attempted earlier in this game and was now entering the field with eight seconds left in the game. The kicking team lined up for the 47-yard attempt. The snap and the hold were good. The ball flew skyward toward the beseeching, outstretched arms of the goalposts. Closer and closer it came, then sailed on by, two feet outside the right upright. The New York Giants were the Super Bowl champions.

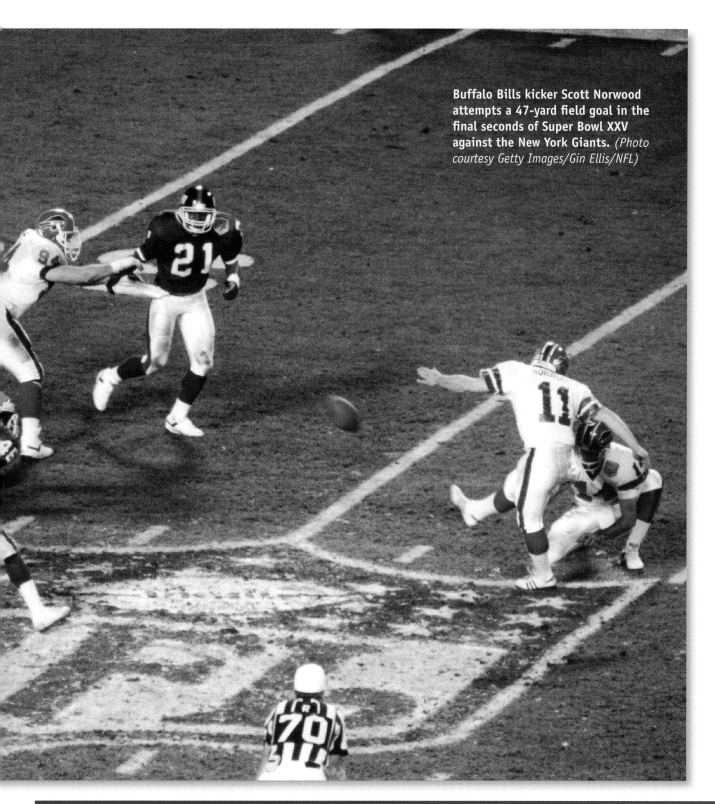

Buffalo Bills kicker Scott Norwood attempts a 47-yard field goal in the final seconds of Super Bowl XXV against the New York Giants. *(Photo courtesy Getty Images/Gin Ellis/NFL)*

That is the play that will always be remembered, but there were many other seminal moments that affected the outcome of the game. It is often asserted that the Giants dominated because of their time-of-possession advantage of approximately 40 minutes to the Bills' 20. What is not noted is that in every close game we played during that season, a similar time-of-possession advantage went to our opponent. That is because the Bills' fast-paced no-huddle offense resulted in either our scoring very quickly or being off the field quickly following a punt. In a hard-fought 17–13 triumph over the Giants at the Meadowlands on December 15, the time-of-possession difference had been very similar to what it was in the Super Bowl.

Midway through the second quarter, with Buffalo leading 10–3, the Giants were backed up at their own 7-yard line. Quarterback Jeff Hostetler dropped back to pass, but before he could get rid of the ball, Bruce Smith was upon him, forcing a fumble in the end zone. The scramble was on for possession of the ball, and in the process Hostetler tripped over the feet of a teammate. He went sprawling headlong and, fortuitously for him, landed directly upon the bouncing pigskin. It was a safety, and the Bills scored two points as a result. Had we recovered, it would have been a seven-pointer, enough so that there would have been no need for that field-goal attempt in the dying seconds of the game.

The safety had given the Bills a 12–3 lead, but the Giants narrowed the gap on their last possession of the first half. With 3:49 on the clock, they began a drive from their own 13. Nine plays later, facing a third-and-10 at our 14, Hostetler found wide receiver Stephen Baker in the end zone to bring his team to within two points at the half.

The New Yorkers kept rolling in the third quarter. They received the kickoff, and this time, while taking 10 minutes off the clock, they covered 75 yards on a march that culminated with Ottis Anderson's one-yard plunge. There had been 16 plays on that drive, but the killer as far as the Bills were concerned came on a third-and-13 at our 32. It was there that Hostetler completed a six-yard pass over the middle to wide receiver Mark Ingram. The Bills tackled him—too well! Linebacker Darryl Talley and cornerback Nate Odomes struck hard, but they succeeded primarily in knocking each other off the tackle. Ingram covered an additional eight yards—enough for a first down—before being stopped by cornerback James Williams. Anderson scored moments thereafter, and the Giants were back on top, 17–12.

We fought back and regained the lead early in the fourth quarter when Thurman Thomas blasted up the middle, broke two tackles, and sprinted 31 yards to a touchdown, giving us a 19–17 advantage. The back-and-forth continued, and once again it was the Giants turn. On a 14-play drive, they moved all the way from their own 23 to a fourth-and-goal at the Buffalo 3, setting up a 21-yard Matt Bahr field goal, making it Giants 20, Bills 19.

The stage was set for the Bills' final drive in the waning moments of the game, the one that finished with Norwood's ill-fated kick. Although Scott is always

Game Details

New York Giants 20 • Buffalo Bills 19

Bills		3	9	0	7	**19**
Giants		3	7	7	3	**20**

Date: January 27, 1991

Team Records: Bills 13–3, Giants 13–3

Scoring Plays:

NY—FG Bahr 28 yards

BUF—FG Norwood 23 yards

BUF—TD D. Smith 1-yard run (Norwood PAT)

BUF—Safety B. Smith tackled Hostetler in end zone

NY—TD Baker 14-yard pass from Hostetler (Bahr PAT)

NY—TD Anderson 1-yard run (Bahr PAT)

BUF—TD Thomas 31-yard run (Norwood PAT)

NY—FG Bahr 21 yards

remembered for that missed field goal, it is well to note that the following year, when the Bills returned to play in Super Bowl XXVI, the margin of victory in three of our games along the way was provided by Norwood's successful field-goal attempts. That included the one he made in the AFC Championship Game when the Bills won their way back into the Super Bowl by defeating Denver 10–7.

During his career with the Bills, the margin of victory on 12 different occasions came as the result of field goals made by Scott Norwood.

> **I**'m disappointed at the way it turned out, but I know I have my teammates behind me. I realize what a big opportunity this was. I'm sure it will never get to a point where I'll ever forget it. I had a good plant, and I hit the ball solidly. I kept my head down on it, but I saw the ball wasn't drawing like normal. I've kicked enough footballs to know, and it was an empty feeling watching it hang out there. That's a kick I've made. I know I let a lot of people down.
>
> —BILLS KICKER SCOTT NORWOOD

Norwood's field goal attempt was no good. *(Photo courtesy Getty Images/Dave Cross)*

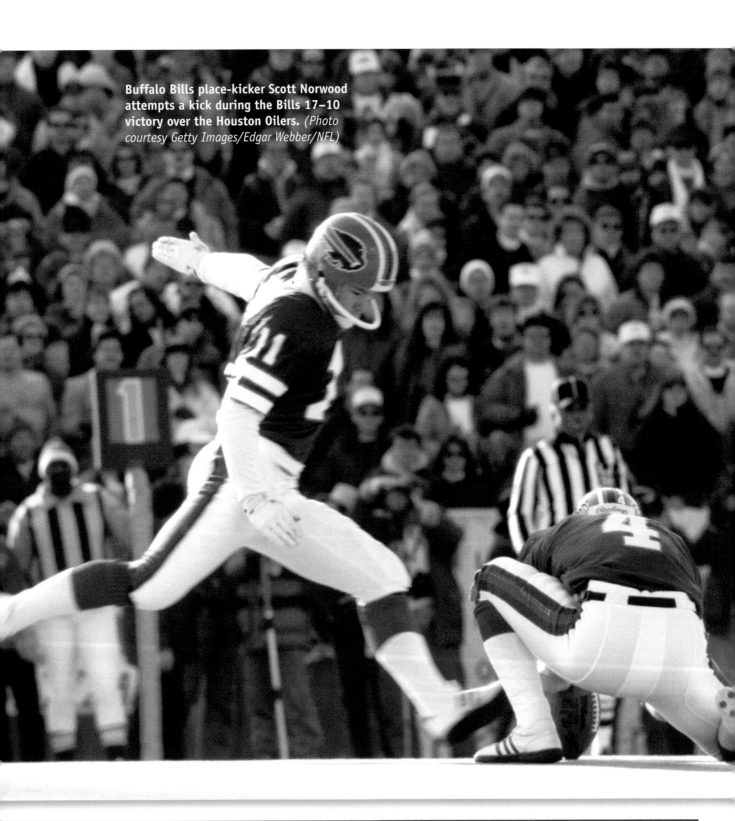

Buffalo Bills place-kicker Scott Norwood attempts a kick during the Bills 17–10 victory over the Houston Oilers. *(Photo courtesy Getty Images/Edgar Webber/NFL)*

November 20, 1988

The Day They Tore Down the Goal Posts

Norwood's Overtime Field Goal Improves Bills to 11–1 and Clinches AFC East Title

How do you win a game in the NFL without even scoring a touchdown? You do it with defense and by blocking kicks. That's how. How do you make your loyal fans go wild with glee when you don't even score a touchdown? You do it by winning a division championship right there in your home stadium. That's how.

It sure wasn't easy, but boy was it ever fun on that late autumn afternoon in Orchard Park. Who cared if rain was falling when the game began? Not those hardy Buffalo Bills fans. There were 78,389 of them in the stands when the opening kickoff occurred. The rain got heavier as the game progressed, and all 78,000-plus of those fans got louder as the contest on the field became ever more tense and exciting.

There were many heroes on the field that day, and a sizeable number of them were not the usual

high-statistics guys. It was tough getting the passing game going in that weather, and Jim Kelly had just eight completions in 18 attempts for a modest 115 yards. Instead, our Bills featured the ground game, totaling 229 yards on 44 rushes. Starting running back Thurman Thomas carried 17 times for 88 yards, but the star in that department was veteran backup Robb Riddick. By halftime, Riddick had only three carries for a grand total of 13 yards, but by the time the game ended he had lugged it 18 times for 103.

We had come into the game sporting a 10–1 record. Just one week earlier on the road in Miami, we had won our sixth consecutive game, breezing to a 31–6 victory over the Dolphins. You never would have known it from the futility we were now displaying during the first half against the Jets. We scored zero points during those first two quarters, and only because of some sterling defensive play by linebackers Shane Conlan, Cornelius Bennett,

Darryl Talley, and Ray Bentley were we able to keep the Jets out of our end zone. Pat Leahy, the Jets field goal kicker, did put one through the uprights, and so at halftime the Jets went to the locker room with a 3–0 lead.

We began the third quarter on a better note by marching from our own 28 deep into Jets territory. Riddick carried four times for a total of 40 yards on that drive, and that got us into position for Scott Norwood to boot a 25-yard field goal, tying the game at 3–3.

Our defense remained stout, and late in the third quarter we took over once again on our own 28. In a reprise of our earlier drive, we advanced again to the Jets' 8-yard line with Riddick carrying on five of the 11 plays in that series, including runs of eight, six, twelve, six, and five yards, respectively. It was early in the fourth quarter when the drive petered out, but a 26-yarder from Norwood gave us our first lead of the day at 6–3. And three and a half minutes later, the Jets got as far as our 23-yard line. Pat Leahy drilled in a 40-yarder for them, and it was now 6–6.

With less than five minutes left, Jim Kelly hit tight end Pete Metzelaars for 35 yards to the New York 25. We were in position to move just a little closer and then kick what almost certainly would be the winning three-pointer, but not so fast! On the next play we fumbled, and the Jets recovered it at their own 30. From there they mustered their best drive of the day, using 10 plays while bleeding the clock down to a mere 19 seconds. At our 23-yard line, the Jets lined up to kick the game-winning field goal. They got the kick away, but big Fred Smerlas blocked it—talk about heroes! The game was going into overtime!

The Jets won the toss. Just our luck. Actually, it was our luck, because on their second play from scrimmage,

> **T**imes have changed for the Buffalo Bills. It's like we're a team of destiny.
>
> —BILLS NOSE TACKLE FRED SMERLAS

> **T**hese [fans] are a hungry bunch. They've taken a lot of crap over the years. I'm happy for them.
>
> —BILLS CENTER KENT HULL

Derrick Burroughs forced a fumble that Cornelius Bennett recovered at the Jets 32. Robb Riddick picked up five yards, then seven, then six, then two. We were at their 12, and from there Scott Norwood nailed the game-winner. It was his third field goal of the day and the one that clinched the AFC East Division championship for the 1988 Buffalo Bills.

Pandemonium! Or, as legendary Buffalo Bills radio announcer Van Miller was wont to call it, "Fan-demonium!" The fans—it seemed like all 78,000 of them—poured onto the field, and I'll always remember it as the day they tore down the goal posts.

Game Details

Buffalo Bills 9 • New York Jets 6 (OT)

Jets	0	3	0	3	0	**6**
Bills	0	0	3	3	3	**9**

Date: November 20, 1988

Team Records: Bills 10–1, Jets 5–5–1

Scoring Plays:

NY—FG Leahy 23 yards
BUF—FG Norwood 25 yards
BUF—FG Norwood 26 yards
NY—FG Leahy 40 yards
BUF—FG Norwood 30 yards in overtime

Fred Smerlas

People don't normally remember much about defensive tackles, but Fred Smerlas of course is the exception to that premise. Among the fans in Buffalo, Smerlas was one of the most popular players to ever put on a Bills uniform. And among his teammates, he is remembered with a combination of respect and affection. Smerlas was a character—always ready with a quip, and always ready to take on his opponent. It seemed like he was constantly enjoying participating in the game, and that spirit spilled over onto his teammates. Whether it was his physical output or the words that he was never at a loss to supply, the motor was always running.

Smerlas came to Buffalo in the second round of the 1979 draft despite having played on a Boston College team that didn't win a single game in his senior year. But those who scouted Smerlas all came to the same conclusion about the 6'3", 277-pound defensive tackle—this guy never gave up no matter how far behind his team was. It was that hard-working, never-say-die attitude combined with a fun-loving approach to the game that immediately endeared Smerlas to the Buffalo faithful. For much of the early 1980s, Smerlas—along with linebackers Jim Haslett and Shane Nelson—formed the so-called Bermuda Triangle, the epicenter of the stout Buffalo defense that led the Bills to consecutive playoff berths in 1980 and 1981—the team's first postseason appearances since 1974.

The Big Greek, as Smerlas liked to call himself, had already been selected to four Pro Bowls by the time I arrived in 1986, and he served as the foundation of the defensive line as we developed into a Super Bowl contender. By the time he left the Bills after the 1989 season, Smerlas had played in 162 regular-season games, appeared in five Pro Bowls, and had been selected to six All-Pro teams. Today, Fred Smerlas' name is proudly displayed on the Wall of Fame at Ralph Wilson Stadium.

The field goal that Smerlas blocked was the play I remember most from that day they tore down the goal posts.

Bills nose tackle Fred Smerlas. *(Photo courtesy Getty Images/Manny Rubio/NFL)*

December 26, 1965

Make It Two in a Row

Byrd's 74-Yard Punt Return Short-Circuits Chargers in 1965
AFL Title Game

Exactly one year to the day after beating the Chargers at War
Memorial Stadium for their first AFL championship, the Bills were
scheduled to meet them again—this time in San Diego—for another
go-round. Despite having throttled the Chargers the previous year,
and once again possessing a better regular-season record, the Bills
were installed as seven-point underdogs. As always, the flashy boys
in powder blue were the darlings of the media, and this year's edition
had the advantage of playing on their home turf and having their
superstar wide receiver, Lance Alworth, back in the lineup.

"The Chargers, both years, were the best team on paper in the AFL," recalled
Butch Byrd, the Bills All-Pro cornerback. "Take a look at their backfield—they had
Hadl as the quarterback, Lincoln and Lowe as running backs, Dave Kocourek was
the tight end, and they had Ron Mix at tackle. They were loaded, but I think we were
better. We were absolutely confident that we could beat the Chargers."

Fellow defensive back Booker Edgerson concurred. "The practices we had were
very upbeat. Everybody was relaxed. We had a defense that didn't give up too much
yardage, and we didn't allow too much scoring that year. We figured if our offense
could get two touchdowns, then we were going to win the game."

But scoring two touchdowns with Buffalo's patchwork offense was no easy task.
With the receiving corps depleted by injury (Elbert Dubenion, Glenn Bass, and
Charley Ferguson were all out), coach Lou Saban and offensive coordinator John
Mazur devised a game plan predicated on the use of double tight-end formations. The

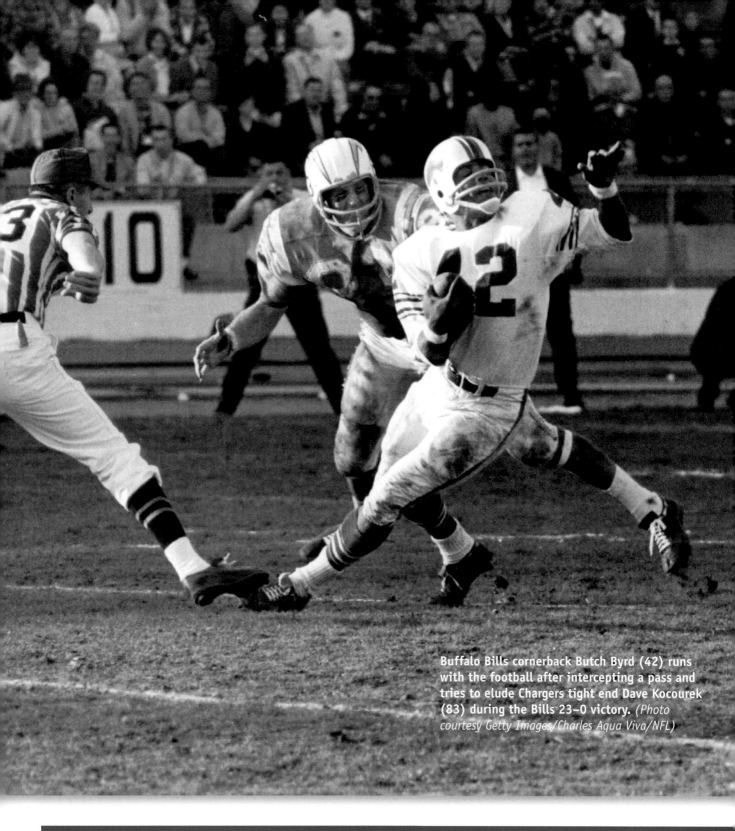

Buffalo Bills cornerback Butch Byrd (42) runs with the football after intercepting a pass and tries to elude Chargers tight end Dave Kocourek (83) during the Bills 23–0 victory. *(Photo courtesy Getty Images/Charles Aqua Viva/NFL)*

hastily put-together strategy proved effective, and reserve tight end Ernie Warlick, who had lost his starting job to Paul Costa earlier in the season, played a major role in the Bills offensive success that day.

Unlike the previous year's game—played on a muddy, cold War Memorial Stadium field—the 1965 Title Game was held in ideal conditions, with the sun shining brightly and game-time temperatures hovering around 60 degrees. It was a beautiful day for football.

After a scoreless first quarter, the Bills took the lead late in the second when Kemp capped a 60-yard drive by hitting Warlick with an 18-yard strike. It was on San Diego's ensuing possession that Byrd made the play of the game. The Bills forced the Chargers into a three-and-out, and quarterback John Hadl was called on to punt. Byrd fielded the kick at his own 26-yard line and, after receiving a key block from Ed Rutkowski to free him to the outside, found daylight as he headed up the right sideline.

"I stepped inside and tried to stay along the sidelines," Byrd explained. "The referee said I stayed in bounds by about an inch." Former Charger Paul Maguire took out Hadl and Dave Kocourek—the last two Chargers—with a single momentous block at the San Diego 20. "Maguire knocked down two guys," Byrd said. "Man, he really hit 'em! That sprung me." Byrd coasted into the end zone for the score, giving the Bills a commanding 14–0 lead.

"That totally demoralized the Chargers," said Bills trainer Eddie Abramoski. Indeed it did, and it seemed the game was going to be a blowout when middle linebacker Harry Jacobs blunted the Chargers' next possession by intercepting Hadl deep in San Diego territory. But Pete Gogolak's 24-yard field goal try was blocked, and the Bills retired to the locker room with the 14-point lead intact.

Gogolak came through early in the third with an 11-yard field goal, extending the Bills lead to 17. Byrd later intercepted a Hadl pass and brought it back to the Chargers 23, setting up a 39-yard Gogolak field goal that gave the Bills a 20–0 bulge going into the fourth. Gogolak added a 32-yarder early in the period to make it 23–0, putting the game out of reach. It was now simply a matter of killing the clock before the celebration could begin.

For the second straight year, the Bills were AFL champions, and the fact that it was the second straight over the favored Chargers in their stadium—and a shutout, to boot—made it nearly impossible for anyone to question just how deserving they were.

"Before today's game," observed Bills defensive coordinator Joel Collier, "San Diego was the best team in pro football. Now what does that make us?"

> That team wasn't nearly as good as the '64 team. But when the chips were down, that team got the job done.
>
> —BILLS GUARD BILLY SHAW

Game Details

Buffalo Bills 23 • San Diego Chargers 0

Bills	0	14	6	3	**23**
Chargers	0	0	0	0	**0**

Date: December 26, 1965
Team Records: Bills 10–3–1, Chargers 9–2–3
Scoring Plays:
BUF—TD Warlick 18-yard pass from Kemp (Gogolak PAT)
BUF—TD Byrd 74-yard punt return (Gogolak PAT)
BUF—FG Gogolak 11 yards
BUF—FG Gogolak 39 yards
BUF—FG Gogolak 32 yards

Butch Byrd

The Buffalo Bills selected George "Butch" Byrd of Boston University in the fourth round of the 1964 college draft. A two-way star at BU, Byrd led the Terriers in rushing in both his junior and senior years, and he was an All-East selection in 1963. The Dallas Cowboys of the rival NFL selected him in the seventh round, but Byrd signed with Buffalo because the Cowboys had already chosen Mel Renfro in the first round.

It turned out to be a good move for both Byrd and the Bills, as the 6', 211-pound Watervliet, Massachusetts, native made an immediate impact, winning the starting right corner position in his first training camp and holding it down for the next seven seasons. He recorded his first interception in just his third game as a pro, picking off Tobin Rote of the Chargers and racing 75 yards for a score. In all, Byrd filched seven enemy aerials during his rookie season, setting a Bills record and earning an invitation to the AFL All-Star Game, the first of five in his career. Along the way he gained a reputation as not only one of the best, but also as one of the most aggressive defensive backs in the league. And he was tough, never failing to suit up in

his entire time in Buffalo, a streak of 101 consecutive games (regular and postseason). He would go on to earn a team-record 40 career interceptions (five of which he returned for scores) and appear in three AFL title games with the Bills (1964, '65, and '66). His 74-yard punt return in the 1965 Title Game set an AFL postseason mark that stood until the AFL-NFL merger.

Byrd was named to the All-Time AFL Team (second squad) by the Pro Football Hall of Fame Selection Committee in 1969. He was named to Boston University's Athletic Hall of Fame in 1980. In 1994, Byrd was presented with the Ralph C. Wilson Jr. Distinguished Service Award for "service to the Bills organization and the Western New York community during his career." He was honored with induction into the Greater Buffalo Sports Hall of Fame in 2008.

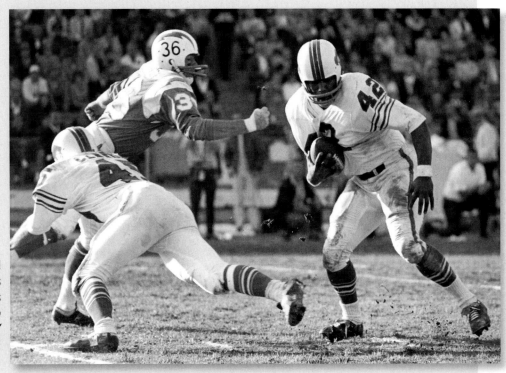

Cornerback Butch Byrd of the Bufflao Bills returns a punt 74 yards for a touchdown. *(Photo courtesy Getty Images/ Charles Aqua Viva/NFL)*

September 30, 1990

Bills Win Wild One Over Broncos

Bennett's Return of Blocked Field Goal Ignites 20-Point Outburst

How do you win a game where the opponent outgains you 410 yards to 197, where they rush for 208 yards to your 64, where they sack your quarterback four times and you get theirs just twice, where your team botches two conversion attempts, where your holder fumbles a snap that aborts a field goal, and where the opponent has a 35-to-25-minute time-of-possession advantage over you?

I'll tell you how, because the Buffalo Bills did just that against the Denver Broncos in Week 4 of the 1990 season. We had won the opener, but the next week in Miami we were awful, losing 30–7. In Week 3 we rebounded with a victory over the Jets, but it didn't take us long to revert to mediocrity when John Elway, running back Bobby Humphrey, and the rest of the Broncos showed up for their game against us at Rich Stadium.

Before it was all over, Humphrey had rushed for 177 yards on 34 carries, beginning with Denver's first possession in which he had seven carries for 41 yards, including his one-yard touchdown run. Denver moved into position

to kick a field goal on their next drive, but linebacker and defensive captain Darryl Talley blocked it. We returned the favor on our ensuing possession when Scott Norwood's 37-yard attempt hit the right upright and bounced awry. One Humphrey run and two Elway passes later, the Broncos were in our end zone again, increasing their lead to 14–0.

By virtue of a hurry-up drive at the conclusion of the first half—which included Jim Kelly passes of 21 yards to James Lofton and 20 yards to running back Donnie Smith—we were able to kick a field goal on the last play, so we trudged into the locker room trailing 14–3.

The second half began just as miserably, but our defense at least began to show signs of life. We went one-two-three-and-punt on our first drive, but then Bruce Smith pressured Elway into hurrying a throw that Kirby Jackson intercepted at our 49-yard line. We were able to advance it just five yards before having to punt. But on the third play of Denver's next drive, Bruce Smith sacked Elway and forced a fumble that Talley recovered for us at the Denver 10. Three plays later, Donnie Smith, on a draw play, scampered 12 yards for our first touchdown of the

Steve Atwater (27) and the Denver Broncos celebrated an early touchdown, but lost to the Bills, 29–28.
(Photo courtesy Getty Images/Mitchell Layton)

Beyond the Numbers

Despite all those statistical shortcomings that I detailed in the first paragraph of this account, what were some of the hidden elements that allowed us to overcome it all? Yards gained dwindle in importance when compared with who wins the turnover battle, so far as statistics are concerned. We forced five turnovers, and although we were guilty of turning it over three times, the team that wins the turnover battle by two or more wins the game 87 percent of the time regardless of who gains more yards. Two of the fumble recoveries we made occurred deep in Denver territory, and we turned both of those into touchdowns. And when you add in Leonard Smith's 39-yard interception return for a touchdown, those three takeaways not only took the ball out of the Broncos hands, but they all resulted in touchdowns for the Buffalo Bills.

But that wasn't all. We blocked two field goals, returning one of them for a score. Given that the Broncos were denied six points by virtue of those two blocks and that one of them turned into seven points for us, means those two plays resulted in a 13-point difference in determining the final score. A team that scores a touchdown on a kicking-game play wins the game 94 percent of the time.

You can have the yards gained. I'll go for the takeaways and the blocked kicks.

---

day. The extra-point snap was off target, so we never got the kick away. Denver 14, Buffalo 9.

The comedy of errors continued. On the first play of our next possession, Thurman Thomas did something he rarely did—he fumbled. Denver recovered at our 19, and two plays later they added another touchdown, extending their lead to 12 points.

We still couldn't muster any offensive fireworks, and when the fourth quarter began, Denver put together a nine-play drive using up 5:40. On fourth-and-1 at our 6, they sent their field goal unit onto the field. But Nate

> It was my best game in a long time. This is to show all those who doubted Cornelius Bennett. You can knock me down, kick me, but don't ever count me out. I had a long struggle with injuries. I think I've had a great season. This is for everybody who wanted to ship my butt out of here.
>
> —BILLS LINEBACKER CORNELIUS BENNETT

Odomes skirted around their left end and blocked the kick. Cornelius Bennett scooped it up and sprinted 80 yards to a touchdown. We made the extra point this time, closing the gap to 21–16.

The pendulum kept swinging ever more swiftly in its new direction. On the second play of the Broncos next possession, defensive end Leon Seals deflected an Elway pass that strong safety Leonard Smith intercepted. (It was a big day for the Smiths of Buffalo!) He rambled 39 yards to pay dirt, and miraculously we had taken a 22–21 lead. It stayed at 22 when this time Norwood's conversion attempt bounced off the left upright.

Again we kicked off. Our super coverage combined with a Denver penalty resulted in their having to start from their own 5. But the first-down snap went awry, causing a fumble that was recovered by Cornelius Bennett at the Denver 2. From there, Kenny Davis took it in for another touchdown. In 77 seconds, we had scored three touchdowns—all of them the result of defense or kicking-game plays.

It became darned important for us to convert the extra-point attempt after Davis' touchdown—giving us an eight-point advantage—because the scoring was not over. The Broncos took over with three minutes remaining, and they covered 70 yards on an 11-play march. The two-point conversion had not yet been adopted by the NFL, so when they added their extra point, we still held a 29–28 lead. That's how it ended. Whew!

That win, ugly as it was, served as a tremendous confidence-builder for our team. We kept on winning, getting better and better in every aspect of play—defense, offense, and special teams. We extended our winning streak to eight straight before suffering a 27–24 loss at Houston, then we soared through the playoffs, first defeating the Dolphins 44–34 and then the Raiders 51–3 in the AFC Championship Game. For the first time in the team's history, the Bills would be going to the Super Bowl.

Did it all start when Cornelius Bennett returned a blocked field goal 80 yards for a touchdown? Yes!

Buffalo Bills linebacker Cornelius Bennett.
(Photo courtesy Getty Images/ Tom Berg/NFL)

Game Details

Buffalo Bills 29 • Denver Broncos 28

Broncos	7	7	7	7	**28**
Bills	0	3	6	20	**29**

Date: September 30, 1990

Team Records: Bills 2–1, Broncos 2–1

Scoring Plays:

DEN—TD Humphrey 1-yard run (Treadwell PAT)

DEN—TD Sewell 2-yard run (Treadwell PAT)

BUF—FG Norwood 37 yards

DEN—TD Winder 3-yard run (Treadwell PAT)

BUF—TD D. Smith 12-yard run (PAT failed)

BUF—TD Bennett 80-yard blocked field goal return (Norwood PAT)

BUF—TD L. Smith 39-yard interception return (PAT failed)

BUF—TD Davis 2-yard run (Norwood PAT)

DEN—TD Natteil 7-yard pass from Elway (Treadwell PAT)

November 23, 1986

Greatest Special Teamer Makes Special Play

Steve Tasker Makes First Block of Illustrious Career

In early November 1986, two weeks before this game against the New England Patriots, I was hired to take over as head coach of the Buffalo Bills. The first personnel move our team made after I came aboard was the claiming of a little-known, low-round draft choice the Houston Oilers had placed on waivers. He was a wide receiver named Steve Tasker. Joe Faragalli, one of the assistants on the coaching staff I inherited, convinced general manager Bill Polian and me that the young lad could help us, so Tasker became a member of the Bills.

Three days after Tasker joined us, we played the Pittsburgh Steelers and came away with a stunning 16–12 upset victory. It was the Bills 10th game of the season, and it was only the third time that year the team had trotted off the field victorious. As modest as that might sound, it was the first time in three years the Bills had won that many games. In both 1984 and 1985, the team finished with a 2–14 record.

Against the Steelers, Tasker still did not know the offensive system well enough to see any action on that side of the ball, but we did find a spot for him on several of the kick-coverage and kick-return teams. His play on those units stunned not only the Steelers but also everyone associated with the Bills, including me. Tasker made three tackles on kick coverage. His blocking and timing on kick returns was sensational. His downing of punts and positioning was textbook perfect. I wondered, could he keep that up? The answer to that was, "No—he would exceed it!"

We lost to the Dolphins the following week, and then we began preparations for the New England Patriots. During the week leading up to that game, I took Tasker aside at the end of each practice and exposed him to a drill and technique for blocking kicks that I taught players during training camp practice sessions. Our punter, John Kidd, had been a college teammate of Tasker's at Northwestern, and Kidd stayed out each day to help lend authenticity to the drill. I was impressed by how soon and how well Tasker seemed to be mastering that difficult technique.

The Patriots had crushed the Bills 23–3 in their earlier season meeting at Rich Stadium, and at the outset of this rematch, it seemed like more of the same. On our second play from scrimmage, deep in our own territory, linebacker Lawrence McGrew sacked Jim Kelly—the first of five sacks we would suffer in the first half—forcing a fumble that rolled out the back of our end zone. The game was 17 seconds old, and the Patriots had taken a 2–0 lead. And it got worse, fast. Midway through the first quarter, Patriots fullback Craig James capped off a short drive with a four-yard run to give them a 9–0 advantage.

While we were busy going one-two-three-and-out, kicker Tony Franklin made a pair of field goals that gave New England a 15–0 cushion. But with just 37 seconds left in the half, Bruce Smith sacked Tony Eason to force the Patriots into a punting situation. Zipping in from off the corner toward a spot 12 inches in front of punter Rich Camarillo's contact point came No. 89. His focal point, his hand placement, his speed, his intuition, and best of all his results—were perfect. Tasker blocked his first punt as a member of the Bills, and it was far from being his last. As a result of this block, we were finally able to put some points on the board. Scott Norwood's 48-yard field goal made it 15–3 at halftime.

It was that blocked punt that energized our team. By halftime we had gained a total of just 24 yards. Our net yards passing—mostly because of the five sacks we had suffered—was a minus-15. We had converted just one of five third-down attempts, and we had succeeded in picking up a measly two first downs in that entire 30-minute period. Things were a lot different when we came back for the second half. Jim Kelly, who had completed just four of his eight pass attempts for 33 yards in the first half, hit on 18-of-24 for 217 yards in the second.

On our first possession, we drove from our own 40 to the Patriots 16. Norwood then booted a 34-yarder that

Special teams standout Steve Tasker. (Photo courtesy Getty Images/NFL)

closed the gap to nine points. Late in the third quarter, we began a drive at our own 19. Four Kelly completions brought us again to the Patriots 16. Another Norwood field goal narrowed their lead to 15–9 just as the final quarter dawned.

Norwood's fourth straight field goal—set up by Fred Smerlas' interception of Tony Eason at the Patriots 17—brought us to within 15–12 with 5:23 remaining. We halted

Steve Tasker "belongs in the Pro Football Hall of Fame," Marv Levy said. *(Photo courtesy of Getty Images)*

We went to New England to play the Patriots, and I wound up blocking a punt to set up a field goal. As I jogged to the sideline after the block, I pointed to Marv, and he smiled back at me. The block showed him that I was coachable and that I was really into special teams and willing to do what it took to be successful.

—BILLS SPECIAL TEAMER STEVE TASKER

their next drive and took over at our own 40 with 3:44 left. Kelly connected with Robb Riddick for a 29-yard gain, then again for 31 yards and a touchdown, and we had our first lead of the day at 19–15. It looked a lot rosier now, but there was to be no happy ending for us on this late-autumn day in New England. In the game's waning moments, Eason completed a 13-yard touchdown pass to tight end Greg Baty. Final score: Patriots 22, Bills 19.

Although we didn't win the game, it seemed that, beginning with Tasker's blocked kick, the Buffalo Bills were reborn that afternoon. One week later, we traveled to Kansas City to play the Chiefs, a team that had defeated the Bills in Buffalo earlier that season. We took the rematch at Arrowhead Stadium, 17-14, and from there we began picking up the momentum that made us the dominant team in the AFC during the years ahead.

Game Details

New England Patriots 22 • Buffalo Bills 19

Bills	0	3	3	13	**19**
Patriots	9	6	0	7	**22**

Date: November 23, 1986

Team Records: Bills 3–8, Patriots 8–3

Scoring Plays:

NE—Safety Kelly fumbled out of end zone

NE—TD C. James 4-yard run (Franklin PAT)

NE—FG Franklin 37 yards

NE—FG Franklin 47 yards

BUF—FG Norwood 48 yards

BUF—FG Norwood 34 yards

BUF—FG Norwood 33 yards

BUF—FG Norwood 28 yards

BUF—TD Riddick 31-yard pass from Kelly (Norwood PAT)

NE—TD Baty 13-yard pass from Eason (Franklin PAT)

Two "Special" Special Teamers

There has never been a special teams player in NFL history like Steve Tasker. I was once told by a renowned head coach from another team that the man on our team for whom they had to prepare for most specifically, despite all the many stars we had on offense and defense, was Tasker. He was the AFC Pro Bowl special team player seven consecutive times. In 1992, he was the recipient of the Pro Bowl's Most Valuable Player Award—amazing for a special teamer surrounded by so many great stars on offense and defense. In a recent vote by journalists who are members of the Pro Football Hall of Fame Selection Committee, they named a hypothetical All-Time pro football team, choosing one man at every position on offense and defense. They also named one former player who was a hardcore special teams player. That was Steve Tasker. He belongs in the Pro Football Hall of Fame.

There were many other outstanding special teams players on the Buffalo Bills during our playoff run from 1988–93. They are too numerous to mention, but one fellow, a defensive tackle (a position not often associated with special-teams play) was once accorded a recognition that merits mention. His name is Mark Pike. PRO Scouting Incorporated, a respected pro scouting service that prepares yearly personnel evaluations on NFL players and teams, has described Pike on more than one occasion as "Best big-man special teams player—ever!"

I agree.

October 25, 1987

Norwood Proves These Bills are Legit

Norwood's Overtime Kick Caps Comeback Win as Real Bills Return from Strike

Two games into what was to have been my first full season as head coach of the Buffalo Bills, the players went on strike. After one week of no games, the owners agreed to go forth with replacement players. It was interesting, but we didn't fare very well, losing two of the three games with that replacement roster. But now the strike was over, and we were heading to Miami with our regular players. Everyone was predicting a shootout, since it would be one of those Jim Kelly vs. Dan Marino hullabaloos. They were right.

It didn't start out that way, however. On their first two possessions, the Dolphins put together touchdown drives of 72 and 64 yards. A pass from Marino to Mark Duper accounted for the first one, and the second came with wide receiver James Pruitt on the receiving end of another Marino toss. On the Dolphins' first drive of the second quarter, they did it again, this time going 83 yards on 10 plays and culminating with another Marino touchdown

pass, this one to tight end Bruce Hardy. It was now 21–0. This was turning into a rout.

With 6:27 left in the first half, we finally began to show some life on offense. With a bunch of short passes, most of them to wide receiver Chris Burkett, we used 16 plays and covered 58 yards to get to the Miami 24. With just six seconds to go, Scott Norwood booted a 41-yard field goal, and the score at halftime was 21–3.

Our momentum continued to pick up as the game went on. After forcing Miami into a three-and-out for the first time in the contest, we drove 67 yards in seven plays to register our first touchdown of the post-strike era. A mixture of Robb Riddick and Ronnie Harmon runs from scrimmage, punctuated by a 33-yard Kelly-to-Burkett pass completion and topped off by Riddick's two-yard touchdown plunge, closed the gap to 21–10. Then one more time our defense forced the Dolphins to punt. A good return by Ron Pitts let us start our next possession at Miami's 45. The Kelly-to-Burkett combo was hot now, and they warmed it up even more as Kelly engineered a drive that included

Bills kicker Scott Norwood's point after the touchdown was good. *(Photo courtesy AP Images/Mike Groll)*

Frank Reich holds for Scott Norwood's kick. *(Photo courtesy AP Images)*

a 16-yard completion to Burkett on a third-and-10 situation, and the drive concluded when those two teamed up again for a 14-yard touchdown. We were back in the game now, and the third quarter ended with Miami leading 21–17.

The Dolphins started the fourth quarter by moving the ball as far as our 28 when Fuad Reviez hit a 46-yard field goal, making it Miami 24, Buffalo 17. It was still that way midway through the quarter, and matters were looking rather bleak as we faced a fourth-and-22 at our own 37. John Kidd's punt arrived at the Dolphins 24-yard line, where it was fielded by Scott Schwedes. The punt wasn't all that arrived there, however. So did our fantastic kicking teams star Steve Tasker, whose tackle knocked the ball free. Our long snapper, Adam Lingner, recovered it for us at their 32. A completion to Andre Reed was good for 29 yards, and two plays later Riddick slammed it in for the tying score.

We kicked off, and once again the men on the kicking teams made a bigger difference than anyone ever acknowledges. Ray Bentley's hit on the tackle forced another fumble, and fellow linebacker Scott Radedic recovered at the Miami 33. We moved to their 17, and on a third-and-5 from that spot, a Kelly-to-Riddick pass was good for another touchdown. It was Riddick's third score of the day. We had taken the lead, 31–24, with just 4:04 left in the game. For Dan Marino, however—and for those trying

Those Special Kicking Teams

Despite our slow start, by the time the game had finished we had outgained the Dolphins 474 yards to their 366. An impressive 345 yards of that total came after the first half. Jim Kelly passed for 359 on the day, and we also rushed for 144 yards as Ronnie Harmon and Robb Riddick shared the ball-carrying chores. It was also a banner day for Chris Burkett, who hauled in nine passes for 130 yards and a touchdown.

Yet with all of the focus that is usually directed toward yards gained from scrimmage, we wouldn't have won this game had it not been for the forced fumbles on kick coverage by Steve Tasker and Ray Bentley and for the recovery of those fumbles by Adam Lingner

and Scott Radecic. Then, of course, there was Scott Norwood's clutch kicking.

Now, long snapper is not a glamour position—that is, not as glamorous as, say, place-kicker. You hardly ever hear about them unless, of course, they misfire on one. Think about it: If a big league baseball player gets a base hit one out of every three times he comes to the plate, that .333 batting average is real good. If a long snapper succeeds in hitting the mark on nine out of 10, that isn't nearly good enough. In all his time with the Buffalo Bills, I cannot recall a single bad snap made by Adam Lingner.

to defend against him—4:04 was an eternity. Marino took his team 80 yards in 11 plays, and when he teamed up with wide receiver Mark Clayton on a 12-yard touchdown pass, the game was tied once again, this time at 31–31. We were going into overtime.

Thank goodness we won the coin toss. Beginning at our own 35 and highlighted by two Jim Kelly completions of 18 yards—first to Reed and then to Burkett—we got all the way down to the Miami 10. Scott Norwood's 27-yard field goal did it. We had come back from a 21-point first-half deficit to pull it out—on the road—in overtime, 34–31.

The strike was over!

> This was a turning-point win for this franchise. What are the odds of coming back to win after spotting Dan Marino a 21–0 lead? In previous years if we had gotten down that deep against a team like this, the game would have ended up 48–0.
>
> —BILLS GENERAL MANAGER BILL POLIAN

Game Details

Buffalo Bills 34 • Miami Dolphins 31 (OT)

Bills	0	3	14	14	3	**34**
Dolphins	14	7	0	10	0	**31**

Date: October 25, 1987

Team Records: Bills 2–3, Dolphins 2–3

Scoring Plays:

MIA—TD Duper 5-yard pass from Marino (Reveiz PAT)

MIA—TD Pruitt 25-yard pass from Marino (Reveiz PAT)

MIA—TD Hardy 2-yard pass from Marino (Reveiz PAT)

BUF—FG Norwood 41 yards

BUF—TD Riddick 1-yard run (Norwood PAT)

BUF—TD Burkett 14-yard pass from Kelly (Norwood PAT)

MIA—FG Reveiz 46 yards

BUF—TD Riddick 1-yard run (Norwood PAT)

BUF—TD Riddick 17-yard pass from Kelly (Norwood PAT)

MIA—TD Clayton 12-yard pass from Marino (Reveiz PAT)

BUF—FG Norwood 27 yards in overtime

Memorable
Moments

January 8, 2000

Music City Miracle

Titans Pull Off Miraculous Defeat of Bills with Desperation Play

The game was over. In the bag. Steve Christie's kick with 16 seconds left had given the Bills all the points they needed to move on to the next playoff round. All they had to do was cover the ensuing kickoff and then, if there was enough time left, defend against an improbable Hail Mary pass. Simple. But what transpired instead has gone down as the most egregious breakdown in franchise history, and it lives forevermore in the professional football lexicon as the Music City Miracle.

The 1999 edition of the Bills had made the playoffs mainly on the arm and—in some cases—feet of quarterback Doug Flutie. But in what was the most controversial personnel move in the team's existence, Flutie was relegated to the bench in favor of Rob Johnson after Johnson played well in the season finale against Indianapolis. And though Johnson led the team to the go-ahead score in the final minute, it was a special teams snafu that was the Bills' undoing.

The Titans dominated play early on as the defense, led by Javon Kearse, held Buffalo to just 64 yards in the first half and provided the first points of the game early in

the second quarter when Kearse forced Johnson to fumble out of the end zone for a safety. Quarterback Steve McNair extended the Titans lead to nine points midway through the period with a one-yard touchdown run, and a 40-yard field goal by Al Del Greco as the quarter ran out put the Bills in a 12–0 hole at intermission.

The Bills finally came to life in the second half, as Johnson led a five-play, 62-yard drive that took them to the Tennessee 4, from where Antowain Smith bulled over to make it 12–7. Early in the fourth, Johnson engineered a nine-play, 65-yard drive that Smith capped with a one-yard plunge, putting Buffalo on top for the first time. Coach Wade Phillips opted to go for a two-point conversion, but Johnson's pass fell incomplete and the score stood at 13–12 with 11:08 remaining in regulation. The Titans continued to fight, eventually reclaiming the lead when Del Greco made good from 36 yards out with 1:48 left. Kevin Williams returned the ensuing kickoff 33 yards to the Buffalo 39. Johnson, with no timeouts remaining, led a six-play drive to the Tennessee 23. Christie then kicked a 41-yarder to put the Bills up by one with just 16 seconds to go.

The Buffalo sideline was agog as the Titans took the field to receive Christie's kickoff, which, barring any major breakdowns, should have been a mere formality. But what they didn't know was that the Titans were prepared for this contingency. Alan Lowry, the Titans special teams coach, had his squad practicing a special play—dubbed the Home Run Throwback for its employment of laterals to keep the ball alive—at least once a week all season. Until now, they had not had a reason to use it. But there was one problem. Derrick Mason, Tennessee's regular return man, was out with a concussion. That forced wide receiver Kevin Dyson into the picture. Dyson had never practiced the play before, but he received an abridged lesson from Lowry as he trotted onto the field.

Instead of squibbing the kickoff, Christie served up a short kick that fullback Lorenzo Neal fielded on the right side of the field. Neal immediately handed off to tight end Frank Wychek, who started forward but, upon reaching the 25-yard line, pulled up and threw the ball across the field to Dyson, also standing at the 25. "I took a hard step out and made sure it was a lateral," Dyson said later. "Once

I caught it, I thought, 'Get a touchdown or good position for a field goal.'"

Dyson proceeded up the left sideline, escorted by a convoy of blockers who guided him untouched the remaining length of the field for a miraculous 75-yard touchdown and a 21–16 lead with three seconds left.

The stunned Bills desperately scanned the field for flags, but none were to be found. However, a replay official in the press box was not satisfied that the play had not been the result of a forward pass—illegal on a kick return—and called for a review. Referee Phil Luckett spent several excruciating minutes reviewing the return from every available angle on the on-field monitor before emerging to declare his findings. "After reviewing the play on the field, it was a lateral."

Del Greco's conversion made it 22–16. Bills fans prayed for their team to pull off a miracle of their own on the ensuing kickoff, but the Titans held.

Tennessee Titans wide receiver Kevin Dyson (87) takes a kickoff return 75 yards for a touchdown. *(Photo courtesy Getty Images/Allen Kee/NFL)*

The loss eliminated the Bills from the playoffs—the team's last postseason appearance to date—and led to the dismissal of special teams coach Bruce DeHaven after 13 years with the club. The game was also the last for all-time greats Thurman Thomas, Bruce Smith, and Andre Reed, as the team released all three for salary-cap reasons during the off-season.

The Titans advanced through the playoffs with subsequent victories over the Indianapolis Colts and Jacksonville Jaguars, earning a trip to Super Bowl XXXIV where they lost to the St. Louis Rams. Buffalo fans could take heart as they watched Kevin Dyson come up one yard short of scoring the winning touchdown in the game's dying seconds.

> **I**t is a play that is going to be remembered for a long, long time.
>
> —TITANS HEAD COACH JEFF FISHER

Game Details

Tennessee Titans 22 • Buffalo Bills 16

Bills	0	0	7	9	**16**
Titans	0	12	0	10	**22**

Date: January 8, 2000

Team Records: Bills 11–5, Titans 13–3

Scoring Plays:

TEN—Safety Johnson fumbled out of end zone
TEN—TD McNair 1-yard run (Del Greco PAT)
TEN—FG Del Greco 40 yards
BUF—TD Smith 4-yard run (Christie PAT)
BUF—TD Smith 1-yard run (pass failed)
TEN—FG Del Greco 36 yards
BUF—FG Christie 41 yards
TEN—TD Dyson 75-yard kickoff return (Del Greco PAT)

A Buffalo Bills player falls to his knees, dejected, after the Tennessee Titans pulled off the last-second Music City Miracle to win the AFC Wild Card playoff game. *(Photo courtesy Getty Images/Al Messerschmidt)*

Wade Phillips

Wade Phillips became the 11th Bills head coach when he succeeded me in 1998. Although he enjoyed a fairly successful stay with the Bills—compiling a 29–19 regular season record and guiding the team to the playoffs in each of his first two seasons—Phillips' name will be forever linked with the stunning playoff loss at Tennessee and the polarizing quarterback controversy that unfolded during his tenure.

Phillips is the son of legendary coach Bum Phillips, and Wade cut his NFL teeth as a defensive assistant on his father's staff with the Houston Oilers from 1976–80. When Bum was hired to coach the New Orleans Saints in 1981, Wade came along as his defensive coordinator. Success did not follow the family to the Big Easy, however, and when Bum stepped down three-quarters of the way through a disastrous 1985 season, Wade took over and guided the Saints to a 1–3 record. He then spent three seasons as the defensive coordinator with the Philadelphia Eagles before moving on to the same position with the Denver Broncos under Dan Reeves. Phillips' first opportunity at a permanent head coaching position came when he took over for Reeves in 1993. He guided the Broncos to a 9–7 record and a playoff berth but was fired after the Broncos sank to 7–9 in 1994.

We hired Phillips in 1995 to replace outgoing defensive coordinator Walt Corey, and he served in that capacity for three seasons until taking over when I retired after the 1997 season. Phillips experienced his best years as a head coach while with Buffalo, taking the team to two postseason appearances and compiling a winning percentage of .604—the second highest in team history (behind yours truly at .615). However, most long-time observers point to the playoff loss at Tennessee as the beginning of the end for Phillips, mainly for the controversial decision to start Rob Johnson in place of fan-favorite Doug Flutie—the starter for most of the season—and essentially igniting the most heated quarterback controversy since Kemp/Lamonica. Phillips was harshly criticized in 2000 for remarks he made on the eve of the December 11 game with Indianapolis when he told reporters that his team was essentially out of the playoff hunt despite the fact that the Bills had not yet been mathematically eliminated.

Things came to a head in January 2001 when Phillips, after receiving orders from owner Ralph Wilson, refused to fire embattled special teams coach Ronnie Jones. This act of insubordination cost him dearly. "Buffalo's special teams record was among the worst in the National Football League last season," Wilson said. "I felt we needed a change and that my request was reasonable. I did not want to release Wade, but his refusal left me with no option."

The resilient Phillips resurfaced two years later as defensive coordinator with the Atlanta Falcons, then he spent three years in the same capacity with the San Diego Chargers. In February 2007, Phillips found himself back in the saddle when he was hired to replace Bill Parcells as head coach of the Dallas Cowboys. The Phillips' coaching family tree that began with Bum has reached a third generation—Wade's son, Wes, serves as the quality-control coach on the Cowboys staff.

December 7, 1975

Fumble! No Wait...

Questionable Call Costs Bills Game and Shot at Playoffs

It is without question one of the most controversial calls in Bills history. In fact, until the term "Home Run Throwback" entered the Buffalo sports vocabulary, "The Fumble" was recognized as perhaps the worst call in a city that had seen more than its share of bad calls over the years. And what makes it all the more galling is that it came against their most hated opponent—the Miami Dolphins, to whom they'd already lost 11 straight—and essentially erased any hopes the Bills had of making the playoffs.

With backup quarterback Don Strock making his first NFL start in place of the injured Bob Greise, the Dolphins had gotten off to a quick start, building a 21–0 lead by intermission on Strock's four-yard run in the first quarter and two touchdown passes to Howard Twilley in the second.

It appeared the Bills were heading down a familiar road as they retired to the locker room bearing a seemingly insurmountable deficit.

The Bills got their act together in the third quarter, however, as O.J. Simpson scored on a 14-yard scamper to close the gap to two touchdowns. Garo Yepremian's field goal increased Miami's lead to 24–7, but Joe Ferguson's 31-yard scoring pass to J.D. Hill made it a 10-point game just as the period was ending. Early in the fourth, Simpson took a short pass from Ferguson and broke free for a 62-yard score, bringing his team to within three points.

The Dolphins began their next drive at their own 25. On second-and-8 from the 27, Strock handed off to halfback Mercury Morris, who was met at the line of scrimmage with a jarring tackle by linebacker Doug Allen. The ball popped free and was recovered by middle linebacker John Skorupan at the Miami 28—or

> **T**he official who made that call should be barred from football. Anyone that incompetent shouldn't be allowed to officiate. I don't care if Commissioner Rozelle fines me $10,000 or $15,000 for my remarks.
>
> —BILLS OWNER RALPH WILSON

so it seemed. To the Bills surprise, referee Gene Barth signaled that Miami was still in possession of the ball, ruling that the play had been whistled dead before the fumble. The whole thing had taken place directly in front of the Buffalo bench and their mercurial head coach, Lou Saban, who went ballistic.

In the brouhaha that ensued, it was ruled that defensive end Pat Toomay had "brushed" one of the linesmen and was penalized 15 yards for unsportsmanlike conduct. Instead of a Bills first-and-10 at the Miami 28, it was a Miami first-and-10 at their own 43.

"We saw the fumble," Saban said, "but there must have been a whistle we didn't hear. The next thing you know, they're marching 15 yards off. It was a crucial call—I couldn't believe they could make a call like that. We didn't play well in the first half, but we had the game under control when that call was made."

The Buffalo defense was still reeling when they lined up for the next play. Strock took the snap and handed off to fullback Don Nottingham, who blew past right defensive end Earl Edwards and romped 56 yards before being brought down by Tony Greene at the Buffalo 1. Norm

Dolphins running back Eugene "Mercury" Morris heads for the end zone against the Bills. *(Photo courtesy AP Images/Jim Bourdier)*

Lou Saban

As a linebacker and captain of the Cleveland Browns championship defenses of the late 1940s, Lou Saban served his apprenticeship in the workshop of perhaps the most innovative and successful head football coach of the modern era, Paul Brown. It was Saban's responsibility to learn and understand Brown's systems, anticipate his every wish, and call the formations that were most likely to, and almost always did, bring about the desired outcomes.

Saban retired before the Browns joined the NFL in 1950, and he paid his dues coaching at the college level before becoming the first head coach of the Boston Patriots of the new American Football League in 1960. His tenure at Boston lasted just a year-and-a-half before he was let go. Bills owner Ralph Wilson hired Saban as the team's personnel director in October 1961 and elevated him to the position of head coach shortly after the season ended. Within two years, Saban guided the Bills to their first-ever postseason appearance, a divisional playoff with the Patriots. Although the Bills lost, the success of that season was an indication of things to come as the Saban-led Bills captured back-to-back AFL titles in 1964 and '65.

In a move that still has Bills fans scratching their heads, Saban departed abruptly after the '65 season to take over as head coach at the University of Maryland. Without Saban, the team's fortunes declined to the point where it suffered five straight losing seasons (1967–71) and numerous coaching changes before Saban was brought back in 1972. It didn't take him long to realize he had a serious weapon in halfback O.J. Simpson, and Saban resolved to make the former Heisman Trophy winner the focal point of the offense. The plan paid immediate dividends as the team improved from 1–13 in 1971 to 4–10 in '72, and Simpson—whose first three pro seasons had been a major disappointment—emerged as the NFL's leading rusher with 1,252 yards.

In 1973, the Bills registered their first winning season (9–5) since 1966, and Simpson entered the record books by becoming the first back in history to surpass the 2,000-yard mark. Saban's ultimate goal of returning to the playoffs was realized in 1974, as the team secured a wild card berth with a second consecutive 9–5 record. However, the dream season ended with a heartbreaking first-round loss to the Pittsburgh Steelers—the eventual Super Bowl champs.

Despite Simpson enjoying what was arguably his best season as a pro (gaining 1,817 yards on 329 carries, plus another 426 yards on 28 catches, and scoring an NFL record 23 touchdowns), the club slipped to 8–6 in 1975 and missed the playoffs. After beginning the 1976 season at 2–3, the emotionally drained Saban resigned.

After leaving the Bills for the second time, Saban held numerous coaching jobs at nearly every conceivable level from high school to Arena. He even switched over to baseball when his old friend George Steinbrenner named him president of the New York Yankees (1981–82) and later scout (1984–87), but he always returned to his first love—football. The ever-fiery Saban remained active as a coach until 2002, when he retired from his last job at Division III Chowan College in North Carolina. He was 81 years old.

Saban passed away at the age of 87 on March 29, 2009.

Buffalo Bills head coach Lou Saban (shown here in 1974) served his coaching apprenticeship with the legendary Paul Brown in the 1940s. *(Photo courtesy Getty Images/Robert L. Smith/NFL)*

Bulaich bulled over on the next play, and the Dolphins led 31–21 with 8:12 to go.

It was all but over now. The Bills had clawed their way back from a 21-point halftime deficit to make it a three-point game only to see a questionable call swing the momentum back to Miami and rob them of a golden opportunity to take the lead and, quite possibly, stop the string of consecutive losses to the Dolphins at 11. Instead, that string was extended to 12 and would eventually hit 20 before it was finally snapped on September 7, 1980.

With the loss, the Bills fell to 7–5 and third place in the division, effectively dashing any hopes of returning to the playoffs for a second straight season. The defeat also obscured another brilliant performance by O.J. Simpson, who picked up 213 yards from scrimmage (96 yards rushing on 18 carries and 117 more on eight pass receptions) and scored two touchdowns. It was Simpson's 12th consecutive game with a rushing touchdown, breaking the previous record held by Baltimore's Lenny Moore.

Game Details

Miami Dolphins 31 • Buffalo Bills 21

Bills	0	0	14	7	**21**
Dolphins	7	14	3	7	**31**

Date: December 7, 1975

Team Records: Bills 6–5, Miami 8–3

Scoring Plays:

MIA—TD Strock 4-yard run (Yepremian PAT)

MIA—TD Twilley 8-yard pass from Strock (Yepremian PAT)

MIA—TD Twilley 1-yard pass from Strock (Yepremian PAT)

BUF—TD Simpson 14-yard run (Leypoldt PAT)

MIA—FG Yepremian 20 yards

BUF—TD Hill 31-yard pass from Ferguson (Leypoldt PAT)

BUF—TD Simpson 62-yard pass from Ferguson (Leypoldt PAT)

MIA—TD Bulaich 1-yard run (Yepremian PAT)

November 9, 1986

The Wayward Wind

Bills Overcome Steelers and 50-mph Winds in Marv Levy's Debut

You might say I came blowing into town in midseason of 1986. After receiving a telephone call from team owner Ralph Wilson and general manager Bill Polian saying they wanted me as their head coach, I came rushing down from Montreal, where I was when the phone call came. It was a windy day when I arrived in Buffalo on Monday, November 4, 1986, and it kept getting windier as the week progressed. By the time we lined up for my first game that Sunday, the recorded wind velocity was listed at 47 mph with gusts considerably more vigorous than that.

I walked into the team meeting room my first day, and sitting in it were fellows like Jim Kelly, Bruce Smith, Andre Reed, Darryl Talley, Kent Hull, Jim Ritcher, Fred Smerlas, Will Wolford, Jerry Butler, Mike Hamby, Pete Metzelaars, and many others whom I would come to like and admire. They were nine games into the season and had won only two of them. In each of the previous two years they had finished 2–14, and yet I perceived a sense of optimism among the young men in that room. In just six days they would be taking the field against one of the best teams in the league—the Pittsburgh Steelers.

The Steelers won the toss, and they elected to receive. Good! We'd take the howling wind at our backs. Scott Norwood's game-opening kick went out the back of the end zone. The Steelers were unable to move the ball and were forced to punt. Their punter, Harry Newsome, was able to get off only a 27-yarder, and we began our first drive in Pittsburgh territory. With the wind in our favor, we covered 49 yards in 14 plays en route to our first touchdown. The scoring play was a three-yard pass from Jim Kelly to Andre Reed. (I think I am going to like those two guys, I mused.) It was one of the few passing-play highlights of the day. With the winds wreaking havoc, we attempted only 22 passes, compared to running the ball on 42 occasions. We racked

Head coach Marv Levy on the sideline.
(Photo courtesy Getty Images/Rick Stewart/Allsport)

Marv Levy served as head coach for the Buffalo Bills from 1986–97. *(Photo courtesy Getty Images/Ron Vesely)*

up 172 yards on the ground, with Robb Riddick accounting for 108 on 25 carries. In what was probably Jim Kelly's most modest performance as a Bills player, his passing yardage total for the entire game was just 76 yards.

On our attempted PAT following Reed's touchdown, the wind blew the ball so far off course that our holder, Frank Reich, had no chance to handle it—or even touch it. We led 6–0. Another Steelers punt into the wind gave us excellent field position just as the quarter ended and, even though we were heading into that gale in the second period, we got as far as their 22, where we faced a fourth-and-3 situation. How about kicking a field goal? A 40-yard attempt into that swirling maelstrom? No way! We decided to go for it, but a pass from Kelly to Jerry Butler got blown to somewhere over Niagara Falls and the Steelers took over. Even though Pittsburgh had the wind at their backs throughout the quarter, our defense continued to sparkle, and we held them scoreless. By the time the first half ended, the Steelers had gained just 27 yards while picking up a single first down.

We had one more possession in the second period, and we put together a 72-yard scoring drive, culminating in

Game Details

Buffalo Bills 16 • Pittsburgh Steelers 12

Steelers	0	0	12	0	**12**
Bills	6	7	0	3	**16**

Date: November 9, 1986

Team Records: Bills 2–7, Steelers 3–6

Scoring Plays:

BUF—TD Reed 3-yard pass from Kelly (PAT failed)

BUF—TD Riddick 5-yard run (Norwood PAT)

PIT—TD Jackson 5-yard run (PAT failed)

PIT—TD Thompson 11-yard pass from Malone (PAT failed)

BUF—FG Norwood 29 yards

Robb Riddick's five-yard touchdown run. Somehow Frank Reich succeeded in grabbing the snap from center this time, and Norwood made the PAT. We led 13–0 as the half ended.

We had the choice in the second half, and since I wanted the wind in the final quarter, we elected to receive. It was the first dumb decision of my coaching career in Buffalo—but not my last. Gary Anderson's kickoff went three yards deep into our end zone, and Eric Richardson brought it out. He got as far as the 17 where, upon being tackled, he fumbled. Mike Merriweather picked it up there and returned it to our 5. One play later, Earnest Jackson ran it in for Pittsburgh's first points of the day. Once again, the restless wind made the snap from center impossible to handle. It was now 13–6.

The wind was really picking up now. Anderson's kickoff went way out and beyond the end zone. Four plays later, John Kidd punted into the stiffest wind I can remember during my 47 years of coaching. His kick went five yards, and Pittsburgh took over at our 29. Five plays later, quarterback Mark Malone hit Weegie Thompson from 11 yards out. They were in position now to tie it up, but the wind that had been plaguing us now helped us as the snap from center on the conversion attempt went fluttering off into the wild gray yonder. We were still on top, 13–12.

On the last play of the third quarter, the Steelers faced a third-and-10 at their own 20. Malone connected with running back Rich Erenberg, but it was good for just eight yards. Cornerback Charles Romes made the tackle in-bounds and, as a result, the period expired. The Steelers, now facing a fourth-and-two, would have to change ends of the field and punt into the wind. Had the pass been incomplete, that punt would have been with the wind. Sometimes you get lucky. Newsome's punt was good for 20 yards. We took over at the Pittsburgh 48 and got as far as their 12. Norwood then kicked a 29-yarder to make it 16–12. Yet it wasn't over.

With two minutes remaining in the game, the Steelers began a drive at their own 20. Despite the adverse conditions he was facing, Malone completed four out of six pass attempts as he moved his team all the way to the Buffalo 29. Only 12 seconds were left to play, so Malone sent one flying toward our end zone. Cornerback Rodney Bellinger, who led our defense with 10 tackles during the game, added to his outstanding performance by darting in to intercept it at our 1-yard line and preserve our victory.

Like Something Out of the Movies

When I returned home late that Sunday, still exhilarated over the Bills having won my first game as coach, I found myself unable to wind down enough to fall asleep. I tuned my television set to the Turner Classic Movies channel and mellowed out by viewing, for at least the hundredth time, Humphrey Bogart in *Casablanca*. The final lines in the movie struck home for me. As Bogart (known as Rick in the movie) strolled into the foggy night, he spoke to the man accompanying him. It was Louie the police chief, played by Claude Raines. These were Bogie's immortal words: "Louie, I think this is going to be the beginning of a beautiful friendship." I thought about those men on the Buffalo Bills roster whose names and faces I was still trying to coordinate, and I realized that, yes indeed, this was the beginning of a beautiful friendship.

Bibliography

Books

Abramoski, Eddie, and Milt Northrop. *Tale of the Tape: A History of the Buffalo Bills from the Inside.* Orchard Park, New York: The Buffalo Bills, Inc. 2002.

Carroll, Bob, Michael Gershman, David Neft, and John Thorn. *Total Football II: The Official Encyclopedia of the National Football League.* New York, New York: HarperCollins. 1997.

DeLamielleure, Joe, and Michael Benson. *Joe D's Tales from the Buffalo Bills.* Champaign, Illinois: Sports Publishing, LLC. 2007.

Felser, Larry. *The Birth of the New NFL: How the 1966 NFL/AFL Merger Transformed Pro Football.* Guilford, Connecticut: The Lyons Press. 2008.

Gillette, Gary, Pete Palmer, Ken Pullis, Sean Lahman, and Matthew Silverman. *The ESPN Pro Football Encyclopedia (First Edition).* New York, New York: Sterling Publishing Co., Inc. 2006.

Levy, Marv. *Where Else Would You Rather Be?* Champaign, Illinois: Sports Publishing, LLC. 2004.

MacCambridge, Michael. *America's Game: The Epic Story of How Pro Football Captured a Nation.* New York, New York: Random House, 2004.

Maiorana, Sal. *Relentless: The Hard-Hitting History of Buffalo Bills Football.* Lenexa, Kansas: Quality Sports Publications. 1994.

Maxymuk, John. *The 50 Greatest Plays in New York Giants Football History.* Chicago, Illinois: Triumph Books. 2008.

Miller, Jeff. *Going Long: The Wild 10-Year Saga of the Renegade American Football League in the Words of Those Who Lived It.* New York: McGraw-Hill. 2003.

Miller, Jeffrey J. *Rockin' the Rockpile: The Buffalo Bills of the American Football League.* Toronto, Ontario: ECW Press. 2007.

Schultz, Randy. *Legends of the Buffalo Bills.* Champaign, Illinois: Sports Publishing, LLC. 2003.

Smith, Robert L. *A View Through the Lens of Robert L. Smith: The Buffalo Bills Photos 1960–1995.* Elma, New York: RLS Publishing. 1996.

Tasker, Steve, and Scott Pitoniak. *Steve Tasker's Tales From the Buffalo Bills.* Champaign, Illinois: Sports Publishing, LLC. 2006.

Tobias, Todd. *Charging Through the AFL: Los Angeles and San Diego Chargers Football in the 1960s.* Paducah, Kentucky: Turner Publishing Company. 2002.

Newspapers

Buffalo Courier-Express
Buffalo Evening News
The Dallas Morning News
Jacksonville Times-Union
Niagara Gazette
The New York Times
The Washington Post

Periodicals

Buffalo Bills Media Guides (1960-present)
Buffalo Fan
Sports Illustrated
Time

Internet Sites

Buffalo Bills (www.buffalobills.com)
National Football League (www.nfl.com)
Pro Football Hall of Fame (www.profootballhof.com)
Professional Football Researchers Association
(www.profootballresearchers.org)